A NEW DAY, A NEW LIFE

A Guided Journal

William Cope Moyers
with Jodie Carter

HAZELDEN

Hazelden
Center City, Minnesota 55012
hazelden.org

ISBN: 978-1-59285-551-3

Editor's note
The names, details, and circumstances may have been changed to protect the privacy of those mentioned in this publication.

This publication is not intended as a substitute for the advice of health care professionals.

Alcoholics Anonymous, AA, and the Big Book are registered trademarks of Alcoholics Anonymous World Services, Inc. All page references to *Alcoholics Anonymous* (the Big Book) correspond to the fourth edition.

12 11 10 09 08   1 2 3 4 5 6

Cover and interior design by David Spohn
Typesetting by BookMobile Design and Publishing Services

A special thanks to Cynthia Orange for her tireless assistance in creating this inspirational text.

Preface

In August 1989, my mother came to visit me in the psychiatric ward of a hospital in New York City, where I was confined following a fifteen-year struggle against alcohol and other drugs. She brought with her bottles of spring water, peanuts and crackers, and a three-subject Mead notebook with a $1.79 price tag stuck on the blue cover.

"Maybe you'll want to put down your thoughts and experiences," she offered, trying to sound resolute and hopeful, but I could hear the pain in her voice. It's a harsh reality for any mother to accept that her first-born son is an alcoholic and a drug addict. "You've always had a talent for expressing yourself. I hope this notebook will help you through the challenges you face," she said.

At first I didn't know what to do with the notebook. Sitting in that psych ward, I was emerging from the fog of an addiction that had numbed me to the real world for too long. My perceptions were raw, confused, and tangled up in the shock that my entire world had collapsed on top of me. I was numb with shame.

The notebook sat unopened for a few days. When I wasn't in group therapy, all I could do was stare out the barred window and try to figure out what had happened to me. And then one day, suddenly, I picked up the notebook and began to write:

> *One week has passed since I crawled into this prison, one week filled with despair, frustration, anger, fear, uncertainty, and a sense of having failed everyone I know, including myself. It wasn't easy coming here. It was even tougher to admit that my disease was drug addiction. But a week later, I am still intact and alive. I am sober, and that is good. Physically my body is healing. I feel good.*

Soon I was scribbling down my experiences with the new people, places, and things that were part of my day-to-day existence in the psych ward. I described the unfamiliar thoughts, ideas, and concepts about my illness and my recent recovery from it. For fifteen years, alcohol and other drugs had defined my life. Once I was free from their grip, a roller coaster of emotions washed over me. Every day I wrote in my journal, sometimes just a paragraph or two, and other times page after page. Even when I was drained, emotionally or physically, I usually found time to jot down a couple of key phrases or a short "to do" list:

> *Heal—my body must live and grow without drugs*
> *Choose another rehab vs. outpatient treatment*
> *Find a job I do well or feel comfortable with*

Renew my ties with my family
Decide who I love
Find my friends
Find my religion
Write all the time

The old blue-covered journal from the psych ward is a record of that part of my journey. I've been writing in a journal ever since.

I wrote my way from the psych ward through four treatments in the next five years—through the utter despair of multiple relapses and fleeting "maybe this time" aspirations to stay sober. I recorded the tidbits of wisdom that my sponsors told me, and my own words about what I heard a newcomer say in a Twelve Step meeting. Later on, years into my sobriety, I put my pen to paper to describe and record the joy I felt when each of my three children was born, and my sadness when my grandmother Mimi died. In dismay, I wrote about my fear and anger after being diagnosed with cancer. A year later, my journal reflected the unguarded gratitude of being declared cancer-free. Subtle moments of glory—the exuberant awe of seeing a bald eagle soar in the summer sky, or the inner sense of serenity when watching snow fall—made their way into my journal.

Ten years sober in 2004, those journal entries became the touchstones that helped to guide me in writing my memoir, *Broken: My Story of Addiction and Redemption*. Without an accurate "real time" recording of what I had experienced during the long and often arduous journey on the road of recovery, I'm certain the book could never have been written. Certainly my story would not have resonated with thousands of other readers whose experiences are so similar to mine.

But more than anything, those thousands of words and sentences and paragraphs and pages remain a potent and heartfelt reminder to me of what it was like, what happened, and what it's like now, which the Big Book of Alcoholics Anonymous reminds all of us are the crucial ingredients of recovery. Looking back over my own recovery that began in the psych ward in 1989, I marvel at how far I've come and how far I've still got to go, one journal entry and one day at a time.

I hope that you, too, will take the same perspective on your journey in recovery. That first year free from alcohol or other drugs may seem daunting, in part because it is! "Life on life's terms" is never easy. But by following the clear guidance offered in this journal, along with your own words of insight and experience, I'm confident your steps on the road of your recovery will lead in the direction of help and healing. The rest of your life is ahead of you. Trust the process. And stay the course.

Introduction

If you are reading this, it's likely that you have decided to create a healthy, rewarding life—and that alcohol and other drugs are undermining your best efforts at achieving this goal. If so, you are not alone. Millions of people have already faced the disease of alcohol and drug addiction and have learned the "secret steps" to recovery. Worldwide, people are using these steps every day to improve the quality of their lives. The secret is that these steps are not a secret at all. Until 1935, there was no known addiction treatment that worked. But in that year, Bill W. and Dr. Bob started a group called Alcoholics Anonymous (AA) and eventually wrote the Twelve Steps to offer simple, straightforward principles—or basic steps—that any person could follow to transform his or her life, to achieve the spiritual fitness needed to keep the disease of addiction at bay.

Working the Twelve Steps will help you preserve your recovery and your life during this first critical year. No matter what your age, whether you have been through addiction treatment or not—this journal will provide the information and inspiration that will prepare you for many of the uncertainties and challenges you will encounter each day of your new life in recovery.

This 365-day journal starts with a five-day introduction to recovery, which presents ways you can make your living environment safe so that you can focus on working the Twelve Steps of recovery. The Twelve Steps of Alcoholics Anonymous are quoted below.*

1. We admitted we were powerless over alcohol—that our lives had become unmanageable.

2. Came to believe that a Power greater than ourselves could restore us to sanity.

3. Made a decision to turn our will and our lives over to the care of God *as we understood Him.*

4. Made a searching and fearless moral inventory of ourselves.

5. Admitted to God, to ourselves, and to another human being the exact nature of our wrongs.

6. Were entirely ready to have God remove all these defects of character.

7. Humbly asked Him to remove our shortcomings.

8. Made a list of all persons we had harmed, and became willing to make amends to them all.

*The Twelve Steps of Alcoholics Anonymous are reprinted from *Alcoholics Anonymous,* 4th ed. (New York: Alcoholics Anonymous World Services, Inc.), 59–60.

9. Made direct amends to such people wherever possible, except when to do so would injure them or others.

10. Continued to take personal inventory and when we were wrong promptly admitted it.

11. Sought through prayer and meditation to improve our conscious contact with God *as we understood Him,* praying only for knowledge of His will for us and the power to carry that out.

12. Having had a spiritual awakening as the result of these steps, we tried to carry this message to alcoholics, and to practice these principles in all our affairs.

The remaining 360 days of the journal are broken into 30-day segments. The first 30-day segment covers Step One, the second 30-day segment covers Step Two, and so on. Each day of this journal includes a message of guidance, questions for you to contemplate and write about, and also a recovery saying or a quote, many of which come from anonymous recovering people. This journal is organized to direct you through the challenges you will face at different points in recovery. If you are not connecting with the topic of the day, you can skip to another point in the journal to find another topic. But keep in mind that this journal progresses just as recovery progresses, so it's best to follow it just as it's organized: day by day.

In the back of this journal is a video with inspirational guidance from others on their own personal journey of recovery from addiction. Also included are video discussion questions for you to think about and share with others. You might want to watch this video before you begin working through the journal. Revisit the video anytime you feel confused or alone, or when you need guidance or encouraging words.

Why Should You Listen to the Wisdom Offered in This Journal?
Each day of this journal is written with specific strategies in mind—including adult learning, relapse prevention, and long-term recovery models—which represent the latest evidence-based practices that are proven to help people recover from addiction.

The educational messages in this journal are based on current brain research, which now shows that addiction is not a matter of any person's strength, moral character, willpower, or weakness. Addiction has to do with brain chemistry and the way an addict's brain is "wired."

Does the following story sound familiar? When you first started using, you quickly discovered that when it comes to alcohol and other drugs, if a little feels good, then more must feel even better. Your friends could go out and have "just one drink," but you drank until you couldn't remember how you got home. Others drank socially, but the first time you got drunk or used drugs, you suddenly felt like you fit into the world. For others it was just a small high, but for you it was the best feeling you'd ever experienced. After repeated use of alcohol or other drugs, you quickly built up a tolerance and needed more to get high. Soon you had to use just to feel "normal." This happened because your brain had stopped producing neurotransmitters, such as dopamine and endorphins, on its own. All of a sudden, the normal things in life—a smile from a friend, a funny movie, your favorite sport, a great dinner—didn't make you happy anymore. Your brain was conditioned to rely on the substance to feel good.

If you are an addict, you have experienced this progression of the disease of addiction. It's likely that your life has become impossible and that you have risked losing everything that you value.

Working the Twelve Steps will allow you to get your life back. It will help you improve your relationships with yourself, with others, and with life on this planet. As you grow stronger in recovery throughout this first year, your capacity for introspection and your ability to reach out to others will heighten. This is the path of the Twelve Steps: Steps One through Three prepare you for change. Steps Four through Nine move you to action. And Steps Ten through Twelve focus on your ongoing recovery and service to others.

Why Should You Take the Time to Write in This Journal?

In early Twelve Step recovery, people are encouraged to tell their story as a way to openly and honestly acknowledge their powerlessness over their addiction. As they work the Steps, this story unfolds further when they take stock of themselves and their behavior. A journal can be a valuable tool in this reflective and introspective process because it helps you acknowledge and accept these truths, without judgment. Recording your history in a journal better prepares you to interact honestly with others in peer recovery groups, and with your family and friends.

Keeping a journal makes particular sense for those who participate in Twelve Step recovery programs. Letting go, "turning over" what you cannot change, changing what you can, acknowledging your weaknesses, and celebrating your strengths are all important aspects of Twelve Step recovery. A journal is a safe place where you can record those changes, let go of your fears, and express confusion, anger, doubt, remorse, and joy. A journal is a constant friend that accepts your negative and positive feelings unconditionally. It is also a place where you can describe and track your emotional and spiritual progress. When you look back, you will be able to see patterns in the way you react to life's challenges.

Growth is what the first year of recovery is all about. As challenging as those first days, weeks, and months may be, the rewards are plentiful. You can expect to experience an acceptance of and release from a painful past, and a renewed sense of hope about a future free from the bondage of addiction. Along the way, you will find yourself move from selfishness and self-pity to compassion and a desire to help others. As you let go of fear and insecurity, you will discover the personal fulfillment that you have been seeking. If this sounds good, then turn to the next page and begin your journey in the first year of recovery.

Start Fresh

DAY 1 TO DAY 5

Create a Safe Space

Your first recovery action step is to "trash your stash": clear your living environment of every last bit of alcohol or other drugs. Get rid of any materials (posters, music, shot glasses, phone numbers of using friends) that remind you of drinking or using. Don't do this alone. Ask your spouse, partner, sober friend, or supportive family member for help.

You might be tempted to save part of your stash. Realize that this thinking will set you up for certain failure. Get rid of *all* your stash, and trust that you can let go of the need to control your life by using substances.

Write down the name of a sober person you can trust. Contact this person and schedule a time within the next twenty-four hours to meet to get rid of your stash. It's hard, but you can do it.

....

....

....

....

....

....

....

....

....

"I will take my recovery journey one Step at a time. The goal is to avoid taking the first drink or first hit and to stay sober one day at a time."

Find a Local Twelve Step Meeting

Alcoholics Anonymous (AA) or Narcotics Anonymous (NA) Twelve Step meetings offer a fellowship where recovering people share their experience, strength, and hope. Going to Twelve Step meetings is especially important during the first year of recovery. You, like many others, may feel isolated and lonely, as though you don't belong anywhere. Using alcohol or other drugs probably made that alienation even worse. What is the best cure for loneliness? Friendship. When you make a connection with others in Twelve Step groups, your feeling of loneliness will fall away. If you have a problem, question, or experience you don't understand, you can turn to a fellow group member for help.

Use the Internet or your local phone book to find a Twelve Step meeting in your area. Make a commitment to go to a meeting during the next twenty-four hours, and plan to go at least once a week. Write down the address of the meeting and the day and time you will attend.

Describe any fears or doubts you have about how the Twelve Step program can help you. Even if you are doubtful, make a commitment to go to a meeting this week with an open mind. When will you attend a meeting this week?

....

....

....

....

....

....

....

....

"Rarely have we seen a person fail who has thoroughly followed our path."
—*Alcoholics Anonymous*

Find a Sponsor

Twelve Step recovery is based on the idea that healing begins when you become willing to share your story with another person. In early recovery, the first person you share with is called a sponsor. When you find a sponsor, you will have a special person who can listen to your story with attentive ears and an understanding heart.

Your sponsor will support, challenge, and help you in times of crisis. He or she will guide you through your Twelve Step work. It is not a sponsor's job to keep you sober or take the place of a trained counselor; it is your sponsor's job to hold you accountable and assist you in building a healthy lifestyle.

When you attend your first Twelve Step meeting, make sure you don't leave without finding a temporary sponsor that is your same gender. A few people in your meeting will likely offer to be your temporary sponsor, but make sure you ask for help if you need it.

Your temporary sponsor will help guide you through the first few weeks or months of recovery. After you get to know people in your meeting better, you may choose a different sponsor who fits your needs better. But right now, make sure you find a temporary sponsor.

Write the name and phone number of that person here. Program his or her phone number into your cell phone or keep it in your wallet. Describe how you feel about having someone to help you with recovery.

....

....

....

....

....

....

"When the student is ready, the teacher will appear."
—Zen Proverb

Understand the Science of Addiction

Research has shown that addiction is not a matter of an individual's strength, moral character, willpower, or weakness. It has to do with brain chemistry and the way your brain is wired. When you use alcohol or other drugs, your bloodstream quickly carries powerful, feel-good chemicals called neurotransmitters to your brain, causing you to feel high. This feeling was so pleasurable that you wanted to repeat it again and again.

Eventually your body got used to the drug and needed more in order to feel high. Eventually your brain stopped producing feel-good neurotransmitters on its own. Ordinary things like good food, a sunny day, or making a friend laugh no longer made you happy. Your body had become a hostage to the drug, and you could not feel happy—or even normal—without it.

Your body was chemically out of balance, and your need to use was more powerful than your best intentions to quit. Because you couldn't quit, your drug use became progressively worse.

Can you relate to this description of how addiction progresses? Take a few minutes to reflect on your first use of alcohol or other drugs. How did your drug use progress? When did you notice that you needed the drug just to feel normal?

....

....

....

....

....

....

....

"A little knowledge that acts is worth infinitely more
than much knowledge that is idle."
—Kahlil Gibran

Plan Your Day

In early recovery, you cannot be around any mood-altering substances. To stay safe, you will need to plan your day to avoid *all* people, places, and things that could cause you to use alcohol or other drugs. It's extremely important for you to stay away from bars or other places that remind you of using.

Don't fool yourself into thinking you can drink or use like your nonaddicted friends. You can't. Your brain is wired differently. Walking into a bar or meeting your using friends at a park is a "slippery slope" that will lead right back to drug use. Nonaddicts can have one drink and go home. For addicts, one drink can easily turn into ten.

Think about the slippery places where you previously used alcohol or other drugs. Did you use when you were home alone? With friends? First thing after waking up in the morning? At concerts? Before or during a date? After payday?

List these slippery places and make a commitment to avoid them at all costs. Instead of going to a bar or over to a using friend's house, write out a plan to go to a Twelve Step meeting, connect with a sober friend, or go to a coffee shop or a bookstore.

....

....

....

....

....

....

....

....

*"Planning my day is one big step I can take to remove the opportunity
to drink or use other drugs."*

Find a New Sense of Power

DAY 6 TO DAY 35

Admit Powerlessness

Step One: "We admitted we were powerless over alcohol—that our lives had become unmanageable."

To admit to being powerless over anything is a difficult and humbling experience. Admitting powerlessness may feel like you're giving up the idea that you can work your way out of addiction. In reality, you're admitting that you can't control your alcohol and other drug use. You aren't wired like a nonaddict. You can't stop after one drink.

There is hope and strength in Step One. Even though you are powerless over the disease of addiction, you are not powerless over everything. True weakness is relying on drug use as a crutch to cope with life. You can become tremendously strong by leaning on your Higher Power and others in recovery, and by letting them guide you.

Use your own words to describe what it means to be powerless as a person addicted to substances. Describe your idea of true strength.

....

....

....

....

....

....

....

....

....

"You have a body that can't handle alcohol or other drugs.
You have a mind that can't give them up. You have a current
spiritual condition that can't do anything about it."

Accept Addiction as a Disease

Addiction is a disease of the mind, body, and spirit. Addiction is not caused by a person's strength, character, or willpower; it's caused by the way an addict's brain is wired. A tough life, failed marriage, or challenging boss doesn't cause addiction.

Is the knowledge that you're an addict or alcoholic enough to keep you from using? Absolutely not. As a person suffering from the chronic disease of addiction, you can't stop using, even when you are faced with losing everything: your job, your family, and your life. This is because you can't control the way your mind and body react to alcohol and other drugs. This is powerlessness.

Learning to accept the disease of addiction is an important part of your recovery. When you accept that you have a disease, you can truly admit that you are powerless against addiction. You can't have even one drink without being faced with losing control over your life.

Describe your experience with addiction. In what ways have your security, job, family, and life been harmed?

....

....

....

....

....

....

....

....

*"Acceptance means being at peace with something
that once deeply troubled you."*

Identify Positive Support

Make a list of sober people you can count on for support. Keep a copy of the list in your wallet, and store each person's phone number on your cell phone or home phone. Make sure you delete phone numbers, e-mail addresses, and other contact information for drug dealers, drinking buddies, or using friends.

....

....

....

....

....

....

....

....

....

....

*"I will live one day at a time. I will make each day one of preparation
for better things ahead. I will not dwell on the past or the future,
only on the present. I will bury every fear of the future, all thoughts of
unkindness and bitterness, all my dislikes, my resentments, my sense of failure,
my disappointments in others and in myself, my gloom and my despondency.
I will leave all these things buried and go forward . . . into a new life."*
—*Twenty-Four Hours a Day,* January 1

Study the Big Book

Alcoholics Anonymous, also called the Big Book, is the core text of Alcoholics Anonymous (AA). It offers real stories of the experiences of real people. Every time you read the Big Book, you will find inspiration, experience, strength, and hope from others in recovery who have been where you are and have felt as you feel. The Big Book explains how working the Twelve Steps can lead any addict to recovery. Bill W., AA's cofounder, drafted the first chapters in 1938, and the book now includes forty-two stories that reflect the cultural diversity of AA groups across the nation.

Read page 25 in *Alcoholics Anonymous.* Take a few moments to describe how you might use this book as an important guide in your life.

....

....

....

....

....

....

....

....

....

"Alcoholics Anonymous *[the Big Book] has all our answers;
it was written by alcoholics for alcoholics.*"
—*The Little Red Book*

Attend a Twelve Step Meeting

There is a story in the Big Book in which a young alcoholic describes how he went from being a top high school student to an alcoholic in college. One day he was so drunk that he walked through a second-story window, falling headfirst onto the concrete below. He survived the fall, but he was prohibited from completing studies at the school unless he attended regular Alcoholics Anonymous (AA) meetings. He reluctantly attended his first meeting, where he expected to meet a roomful of losers. Instead, he was welcomed by well-dressed, happy people who greeted him as one of their own. They offered him practical suggestions and listened attentively. Soon his life began to transform.

Read this story on pages 421–431 in *Alcoholics Anonymous* and attend a meeting as soon as possible. Describe your feelings after the meeting. Did you share the young man's hesitation? Did you share his sense of surprise and relief at finding regular, everyday people at meetings?

....

....

....

....

....

....

....

....

"Many meetings, many chances; few meetings, few chances;
no meetings, no chances."

Learn about Relapse

Remember that addicts—even those with years of sobriety—must never use alcohol or other drugs again. Not ever. That said, some people do slip and use again, even though they have worked hard on recovery for months, years, or decades. Remember that if you do slip, you can stop. Don't give up on yourself just because you made a mistake. There's still time for you to move right back into your recovery. Don't minimize all the progress you've made—go right back to the Twelve Steps and start again. Learn from your mistakes and avoid them in the future. But don't use this as an excuse to think you can use "just one more time." Any use—even one time—is very serious. Avoid taking that first drink or hit at all costs.

Work with your sponsor or recovery group to form a relapse response plan. Your plan might look like this: If I slip, I will

- stop using
- call my sponsor immediately
- go to a Twelve Step meeting within the next twenty-four hours

Write down your individual relapse response plan here. Keep a copy in your wallet so you have it with you at all times.

....

....

....

....

....

....

"I have the courage to change."

Stay Away from All Mood-Altering Substances

Chemically dependent people don't crave a particular drug; they crave the euphoria that the drug produces. They are addicted to the *feeling* of intoxication, not to the drug itself. This means you can easily become addicted to any mood-altering chemical that gives you the high you seek.

You may think, "I'm going to quit using meth. I'll just have a few drinks instead." This is dangerous thinking. If you try to get high by using a different mood-altering chemical, you will only end up in relapse. Eventually, you'll go back to using the original substance of choice because your brain craves the high. To recover, you must stop using *all* mood-altering chemicals.

Describe the mood-altering chemicals you have felt tempted to use. Maybe you've thought about replacing hard liquor with beer, or taking prescription medications instead of heroin. It's natural to want to replace the high that you are used to. Make sure you are open and honest as you talk with your sponsor about these and other temptations that could cause a relapse.

....

....

....

....

....

....

....

....

"Nothing is so bad that a drink won't make it worse."

Let Go of Shame and Guilt

Once you accept the idea of addiction as a disease, you're no longer baffled by why you're using. You can let go of shame, guilt, and anxiety, and you can get down to the work of recovery.

Think about how the disease of addiction has caused you to feel afraid, sad, angry, or depressed. Were you disrespectful to yourself and to others? Did you lose your job or your driver's license? Did you suffer financial or legal consequences? Did your friends and family suffer as a result of your addiction? This damage is proof that you have the disease of addiction.

Describe the damage you and others have suffered as a result of your addiction.

....

....

....

....

....

....

....

....

....

"I accept that I have the chronic disease of addiction. Now that I understand the disease, I will work hard to heal and repair the damage to myself and to others by staying sober one day at a time."

Find a Higher Power

The Twelve Steps are based on trusting in "a Power greater than ourselves." Some people call their Higher Power God. Your Higher Power can be defined in many ways. Some people find their Higher Power in nature or in a group of recovery friends. A belief in God or religion is not necessary. What is necessary is knowing that you can't achieve sobriety alone.

Describe how you see your Higher Power. If you have trouble trusting or accepting help from others or if you insist on handling things alone, you will probably resist the idea that a Higher Power can help you. If you don't have an idea of a Higher Power right now, write about something or someone that you trust. Whom or what do you have faith in?

....

....

....

....

....

....

....

....

....

....

....

"My Higher Power is a feminist and has a fantastic sense of humor. She knows me better than I know myself and loves me to pieces. The longer I'm sober, the more I turn to her for guidance."

Claim Your Spiritual Power

Even though you are powerless over the disease of addiction, there are things you have the power to do, such as walking away from a bar, making your home a safe, sober environment, and leaning on sober friends and family for help. You have the power to go to a Twelve Step meeting or connect with your recovery group. You have the power to believe that your Higher Power is always guiding you, even when you don't recognize it.

Use your own words to describe how you can be more powerful in your recovery. Do you go to Twelve Step meetings? Do you connect with your sponsor, recovery group, and supportive friends and family?

....

....

....

....

....

....

....

....

....

....

....

"We surrender to win."

Give Up One Drink for One Day

There is a story in the Big Book about a doctor who complained that all the talk at recovery meetings about drinking, drinking, drinking just made him thirsty. He wanted to talk about "important" problems, not about how giving up one drink for one day could keep him sober. However, once he accepted that addiction is a disease, his life became manageable. He discovered that virtually all his problems were connected to addiction.

Read pages 416–417 in *Alcoholics Anonymous.* Describe how you think giving up alcohol or other drugs one day at a time can make your life more manageable. Did many of the problems you once thought had nothing to do with your addiction disappear when you stopped using?

....

....

....

....

....

....

....

....

....

"My whole life depends on not taking that drink . . . Besides, I have promised that Higher Power that I wouldn't do it . . . and I won't break my promise to God."
—*Twenty-Four Hours a Day,* January 7

Surround Yourself with Positive Messages

Write down the Serenity Prayer and place it on your refrigerator, in your bedroom, in your car, on your TV, and in your planner or calendar. If you used to keep beer in your fridge, replace it with healthy water or juice. Replace addictive medications with a copy of the Serenity Prayer in your medicine cabinet. Leave a copy of the Big Book on your nightstand.

Describe a few places where you can place positive messages or other positive items. Be specific. Make a commitment to carry out this action within the next twenty-four hours.

....

....

....

....

....

....

....

....

....

....

....

"God, grant me the serenity to accept the things I cannot change, the courage to change the things I can, and the wisdom to know the difference."
—Serenity Prayer

Embrace the Twelve Steps

The Twelve Steps are the principles of recovery established by Bill W. and Dr. Bob in 1935 when they founded Alcoholics Anonymous (AA). Since then, other Twelve Step groups such as Narcotics Anonymous (NA) have adapted this successful program to help people in recovery. The Steps help you understand the difference between things you have no control over and things you are responsible for. The Steps will help you grow spiritually as you courageously face your shortcomings and make amends for wrongdoings.

The Steps have a spiritual base, but you don't have to be religious to work the Steps. People of all religious faiths, agnostics, and atheists are all able to embrace the Twelve Step program of recovery with no conflict of belief.

Copy the Twelve Steps from pages 59–60 in *Alcoholics Anonymous,* and rephrase each one using the pronoun "I" (for example, "I admitted I was powerless . . ."). Place your handwritten copy of the Steps on your refrigerator, on the wall, or in your car where you will see it often. Think of the Steps as your personal recovery program and revisit them often.

"The Twelve Steps are a simple program for complicated people."

Limit Stress

In early recovery, it's best to avoid stressful situations, if possible. You can't wipe all stress out of your day, but you can try to limit the number of stressful events in your day. Maybe you're tempted to confront a difficult situation with a friend or spouse. Maybe you want to demand a raise at work or confront your landlord. There are always things you can say no to, just for today.

What are some things in your life that are likely to cause you stress? Which of these things can you say no to right now?

....

....

....

....

....

....

....

....

....

....

*"I pray that I may be calm and let nothing upset me. I pray that I may not let
material things control me and choke out spiritual things."*
—*Twenty-Four Hours a Day,* January 21

Deal with Withdrawal

Although it may be hard to believe, most withdrawal symptoms—fuzzy thinking, forget-fulness, anxiety, sleeplessness, clumsiness, emotional numbness, hypersensitivity, flu-like symptoms—are temporary. These will lessen as you spend more time being clean and sober. Try to be patient and remember that the recovery process is allowing your best self to re-emerge. It just takes time.

In the meantime, spend time with your sponsor, recovery group, and supportive friends and family. These people can help you keep a weekly routine that includes a balanced diet and adequate sleep, which will help you recover from any lingering withdrawal symptoms you may be experiencing.

Remember that it's common to feel impatient, angry, or uncertain when you first get sober. Describe how you feel about the idea of a life of recovery. Share this information with your sponsor.

....

....

....

....

....

....

....

....

....

*"Addiction to alcohol has set up a poisoning within our bodies . . . The First Step
of recovery is to recognize our alcoholism and admit our physical illness."*
—*The Little Red Book*

Watch Out for Triggers

Triggers are any situations that could lead you to use alcohol and other drugs. Triggers can be situations that cause challenging emotions, such as having a fight with your spouse or significant other, getting fired from a job, or facing the loss of a friend. Triggers can also be things in your environment that cause you to crave a drink or a hit, such as the smell of cigarette smoke, a beer commercial on TV, the liquor store on the corner, or even a sunny day when your favorite songs start playing on the car radio.

Triggers are normal—the important thing is not to act on them. Instead, call your sponsor or a recovery friend or go to a meeting. Just make it through the first moment, and then the next . . . eventually the trigger will pass.

What triggers have you experienced this week? Describe how you felt and what you did to deal with them. Whom will you call when you feel tempted to drink, get high, or use any mood-altering substance?

....

....

....

....

....

....

....

....

....

"We are defined by what we attempt."

Let Go of the Need to Control

Practice accepting the fact that you are an addict. You have no effective mental defense against the first drink of alcohol or use of other drugs.

Listen to this story: Jamie has been sober for fourteen days and is starting to feel confident in recovery. He starts to think that just one drink at the bar with friends wouldn't be a big deal, so he walks in and orders a beer. While his friends are talking, he downs the drink and orders another. Soon two turn into three, four, five . . . and he winds up home in bed not knowing how he got there.

Why can't Jamie control his drinking like his friends? Describe what Jamie could have done differently. Have you wanted to test your ability to control alcohol or other drug use? Write about the situation and how you handled it. How can you make sure you don't end up like Jamie?

....

....

....

....

....

....

....

....

"I pray that I may be willing to go through a time of testing.
I pray that I may trust God for the outcome."
—*Twenty-Four Hours a Day,* July 7

Review Step One

Step One: "We admitted we were powerless over alcohol—that our lives had become unmanageable."

Step One advises you to accept that you are powerless over alcohol and other drugs. This is not to take away your power but to guide you toward a new way of thinking and to give meaning to your struggle. Once you understand addiction as a disease, you're no longer baffled by why you're using. You can become more comfortable with yourself and with others. You can let go of shame and guilt and start to work toward your ongoing recovery. When you admit powerlessness, you admit that you can't control everything in your life. But you are responsible for the effort you make.

How do you know whether you've understood Step One? You'll no longer be baffled by why you were using. You'll realize the importance of staying clean and sober. And you'll have opened your mind to the spirituality that will heal you.

Write, in your own words, what Step One means to you.

....

....

....

....

....

....

....

....

....

"The alcoholic at certain times has no effective mental defense against the first drink."
—*Alcoholics Anonymous*

Learn from Twelve Step Meetings

Meetings are the backbone of Twelve Step fellowship. People who attend share experiences, strength, and hope, and their willingness and honesty will inspire your recovery. The Twelve Step program works because it doesn't judge, and longtime members are willing to share their wisdom with newcomers. Fellowship is a critical part of recovery. It helps overcome the isolation and loneliness you may have felt in your days of active addiction.

The promise of the program is that those who follow the Steps will find happiness and a new sense of freedom. At meetings, members tell their stories and share how they've failed and how they've succeeded in their recovery. They answer questions, listen, and keep what they hear private.

Describe how you felt after attending a recent Twelve Step meeting. What did you learn? What wisdom did you share? If you haven't gone to a meeting yet, find a local meeting right now. Write down the address and the day and time you will attend.

....

....

....

....

....

....

....

....

....

"Seven days without a meeting makes one weak."

Embrace Your Effort

One of the first goals in recovery is to let go of any shame that ties you to the past, and to embrace the positive work you are doing in recovery today. Many addicts are ashamed of the poor choices they made while using. When you understand that you are powerless over the disease of addiction, you begin to heal and embrace recovery.

Instead of focusing on past mistakes, take a few minutes each day to remind yourself of the good things you've done. Begin to make an honest assessment of your strengths.

Write down some of the positive things that have happened since you started working on recovery. Do you see ways your self-esteem is healing? Do you see ways you are becoming more peaceful and spiritual?

....

....

....

....

....

....

....

....

....

....

"Faith can move mountains. I pray that I may learn to depend
less on myself and more on God."

Avoid High-Risk Situations

It's not uncommon for people in early recovery to return to drug use in challenging situations, such as attending a funeral, a court proceeding, or a meeting with someone who has "pushed your buttons" in the past. These situations can trigger traumatic emotions and memories, and they can increase your risk of a relapse. As a new recovering person, you need to avoid stressful, high-risk situations on a daily basis.

List the stressful situations or people that you are likely to face in the next week. Draw a line through the situations that you can avoid for now. For the situations you can't avoid, talk to your sponsor, supportive family members, and recovering friends to develop a plan to deal with the situation safely.

*"Even when things are stressful, deep down in my heart
I know that everything will be all right, and that my Higher Power
is always with me, guiding me."*

Review Your Schedule

This journal has already asked you to plan your day. This plan should spell out how you will spend your time during every hour of each day. This may sound extreme, but a detailed plan is essential to help you avoid being around people and places that can cause you to return to use. Take some time today to review your plan.

- Are there certain times of day that are difficult for you?
- Are there periods of time when you will be alone?
- Are there events coming up that will be stressful for you?
- Did you plan time for fun sober activities?
- Did you plan time for Twelve Step meetings and talking with your sponsor?

Write down an update of your daily schedule to make sure that you avoid risky people, places, and things, and that you make time to get the daily support you need.

....

....

....

....

....

....

....

....

*"Planning my day is one step I can take to remove the opportunity
to drink or use other drugs."*

Have Fun

Make a commitment to do at least one positive sober activity in the next week. Remember, fun does not need to be expensive. Simple pleasures work too.

Schedule fun sober activities on your calendar and make them a regular routine that you can look forward to. For example, you might decide to meet with a supportive friend every Tuesday afternoon for coffee or tea. You could plan to see a movie on Sunday afternoon, to walk outside on Wednesday after work, or to visit a library on Saturday morning.

List some sober activities that allow you to enjoy the moment. Write down the day and time you plan to treat yourself to some fun.

....

....

....

....

....

....

....

....

....

....

"The past is history. The future is a mystery.
The only time we really have is now—just this moment."

Keep Surrendering

Addicts often resist the idea of powerlessness or turning their lives over to a Higher Power. Like many, you may have put your faith in things like alcohol and other drugs, friends who use, or your own self-will. Addiction clouded your ability to understand that you can't control your use of alcohol and other drugs.

If you are still resisting the idea of powerlessness, you are delaying the spiritual transformation that Twelve Step recovery offers to you. Get started working the Twelve Steps by going to meetings. Grasp a hand extended in support and friendship. Share your story with others. You will discover what millions of others have learned: recovery is a group activity.

Describe any resistance you are currently experiencing. What are three things you can do today to help overcome this resistance? Will you go to a meeting this week? Will you read the Big Book?

....

....

....

....

....

....

....

....

....

"Will I . . . do what I have to do today? Tomorrow may be too late.
How do I know there will be a tomorrow for me?"
—*Twenty-Four Hours a Day,* October 17

Watch for Warning Signs

In early recovery, you are especially at risk for a relapse, or a return to use. Remember that your recovery is very dependent on the fitness of your spiritual condition. Watch out for these warning signs of relapse:

- not going to Twelve Step meetings
- failing to develop a supportive relationship with your sponsor
- believing you can work a good recovery without a Higher Power
- thinking that you can control your use (by having "just one drink," for example)
- believing that staying sober is enough—that spirituality isn't needed
- focusing on the past by wallowing in guilt, shame, and resentments

List the warning signs you experienced in the last week. Remedy these warning signs by talking with your sponsor, meditating or praying, going to meetings, and spending time with people in your recovery group.

....

....

....

....

....

....

....

"Our lives teach us who we are."
—Salman Rushdie

Connect with a Twelve Step Sponsor

If you haven't found a Twelve Step sponsor who fits your needs, make it a priority to find one. If you are having trouble choosing a sponsor, make sure you still have a temporary sponsor until you find someone with whom you really connect. It will take time to develop a relationship with your sponsor, but once you find someone who's right, it will make all the difference.

When looking for a sponsor, choose someone whom you admire, who is your same gender, and who has had one year of continuous recovery. Write down the names of three possible sponsors in your recovery group. Pay close attention to these three people. How does each interact during meetings? With whom could you relate most closely? Who offers wise counsel and listens attentively?

"I pray that my sponsor will help to guide me one day at a time.
I pray that for each day, I will find the wisdom and strength that I need."

Deal with Sticky Situations

Even though you've planned your day to avoid sticky situations, there will be some you can't avoid. For example, you may be required to attend a work event where alcoholic beverages will be served. If you can't avoid a sticky situation, use these coping strategies:

- Ask a supportive sober friend to go with you.
- Talk with your sponsor and come up with a plan to deal with the situation.
- Make an agreement with yourself that you will leave the event early if you sense any warning signs of a relapse.
- Make sure you have arranged a safe ride home in case you need to leave the event early.

Describe a sticky situation that you may have to face in the next few weeks. Talk with your sponsor or recovery group to make a plan to handle the situation safely.

....

....

....

....

....

....

....

"Day after day our sobriety results in the formation of new, positive habits.
As each twenty-four-hour period ends, we find that the business of staying sober
is a much less trying and fearsome ordeal than it seemed in the beginning."
—Adapted from *Twenty-Four Hours a Day,* July 1

Build Self-Esteem

Self-esteem is a feeling of confidence, self-respect, and satisfaction. Acknowledging that you have the disease of addiction can be hard on your self-esteem because you may believe some of the media stereotypes that portray addicts as lowlifes or losers.

Step One helps you move beyond guilt and shame when you accept that addiction is not about strength, weakness, moral character, or willpower. Addiction is about how you're wired, which leaves you powerless over the substance to which you are addicted. You are different from a nonaddict. You can't stop using, even when faced with horrendous loss. Reminding yourself of this powerlessness will help you build the positive self-esteem that is necessary for spiritual development.

Review Step One. Write down the ways your acceptance of powerlessness can help you develop more positive and loving feelings toward yourself.

....

....

....

....

....

....

....

....

....

"See yourself as your Higher Power sees you."

Strengthen Courage

American novelist Ernest Hemingway wrote, "The world breaks everyone and afterward many are stronger at the broken places." When you admit your powerlessness and accept that which cannot be changed, you step out of the way. You let your Higher Power heal the old wounds that, prior to entering recovery, threatened to maim you permanently. You pray for courage to change and improve each and every day, and step by step, you grow stronger than you've ever been.

The first year of recovery is scary business because you don't know what to expect. You may worry about your health, your relationships, your finances, your job, and a host of other things. But being in recovery is about having faith that things will work out, and with faith comes courage—the courage to change and the courage to heal.

Read page 266 in *Alcoholics Anonymous*. Write about ways you find the courage to face each new day.

....

....

....

....

....

....

....

....

....

....

"FAITH = Fear Ain't In This House"

Learn about Denial

Denial is a refusal to admit the obvious. Denial is often at the heart of things when you minimize, rationalize, justify, or blame. When you were using, you may have denied your addiction by thinking things like "I can stop using at any time," "If I were an addict, I wouldn't be able to hold this important job," or "My family exaggerates my problems with alcohol." Your friends and family may also have denied your addiction as a way to protect themselves from the problems it was causing.

Denying your powerlessness affects Step One. Denying your inability to stop using undermines Steps Two and Three. Denying the harm your addiction caused dilutes the integrity of the other Steps and weakens your ability to make amends.

Describe ways you are still in denial about your addiction and the harm it has caused. Talk to your sponsor about what is blocking you. Ask your Higher Power for help as you seek to let go of denial and embrace reality.

....

....

....

....

....

....

....

....

"DENIAL = Don't Even Notice I Am Lying"

*Congratulations for working on Step One! You are begin-
ning to find a new sense of power. If you notice your old
ways and thoughts resurfacing, go back and review the
lessons you learned in this Step.*

Heal Your Mind, Body, and Spirit

DAY 36 TO DAY 65

Believe in a Higher Power

Step Two: "Came to believe that a Power greater than ourselves could restore us to sanity."

In Step One, you admitted you are powerless over using and that your life has become unmanageable. You learned that you're not a bad person, and that you don't have to be alone anymore. It takes courage to take that First Step. Give yourself credit for what you've just done. You deserve it!

In Step Two, you are learning to see addiction as a spiritual problem that requires a spiritual solution. This means you need the help of others; you don't have all the answers. To succeed in lifelong recovery, you will need to find a loving, guiding power you can trust. You can define your Higher Power however you want. A belief in God or religion is not necessary.

Describe your Higher Power. If you have trouble asking for help, you may be resisting the idea that a Higher Power can help you. If you don't have an idea of a Higher Power, write about whom you trust or have faith in.

....

....

....

....

....

....

....

....

"Step Two opens a vista of new hope, when based on willingness and faith."
—*The Little Red Book*

Deal with Addictive Thinking

The key to dealing with addictive thinking is to stop the thoughts before they build into an overwhelming craving to use alcohol or other drugs. Addiction feeds on negative attitudes and resistance to spiritual growth. Watch for signs of self-pity, impatience, blame, rationalization, resentment, anger, and pessimism. These can undermine your recovery. Examples of addictive thinking include the following:

- I don't need to work the Twelve Steps.
- I can have just one drink, and then I'll stop.
- People who go to Twelve Step meetings are losers.
- If others had my problems, they'd use or drink too.

Take a good look inside and ask yourself whether you engage in addictive thinking. Describe the addictive thoughts that hold you back. Talk to your sponsor or recovery group for guidance on how you can overcome these roadblocks to recovery.

....

....

....

....

....

....

....

"Don't believe everything you think."

Survive a Relapse

Relapse doesn't mean you've "flunked" recovery; it's a temporary setback. If you focus on the negatives and get stuck in guilt, shame, blame, and resentment, you put your recovery at risk. Get immediate help and get back to recovery. Research shows that those who view relapse as a serious but alterable mistake are able to restart their sobriety and achieve abstinence sooner. After a relapse, you can make your recovery even stronger because relapse reinforces the fact that you are human. Embrace this humble lesson, ask your Higher Power for strength and guidance, and go to a meeting. Relapse is dangerous territory, so don't get complacent. But you know what to do: stay away from triggers and high-risk situations, practice coping skills, and work the Steps. If you've started using alcohol or other drugs, stop and get help immediately from your sponsor or support group.

Look back over your relapse response plan (see Day 11). If you haven't created one, make a commitment to do it this week. Make sure you list at least two people you will call if you relapse. Make a personal commitment to call at least one of these people immediately if you return to drug use.

....

....

....

....

....

....

....

"Those who slip know they can reclaim the program if they choose.
Nothing is entirely lost and their Higher Power is always there, ready to help."
—Adapted from *Twenty-Four Hours a Day,* December 6

Find Power and Peace

Working Step Two means seeking the spirituality that will give your life strong, steady meaning. When you work Step Two, you will find strength in your faith instead of in drug use.

Consider this story from a recovering cocaine addict: "When I first got into recovery, I was down on nearly everyone and everything. I heard about the concept of a Higher Power, but my self-esteem had dropped so low that I thought it was crazy to believe anything could help me out of the pit I had dug for myself. My sponsor pointed out that for years I'd believed that cocaine and alcohol could help me feel better about myself. I had to admit that she was right. After that talk, I started to think that if I'd been willing to trust a 'lower power' for so long, I might as well give a Higher Power a chance. That day was my awakening."

Read page 43 in *Alcoholics Anonymous.* Use your own words to describe what Step Two means to you. Are there ways you can find power, strength, and peace in your Higher Power?

....

....

....

....

....

....

....

....

"However intelligent we may have been in other respects,
wherever alcohol has been involved, we have been strangely insane.
It's strong language, but isn't it true?"
—*The Little Red Book*

Explain the Disease of Addiction

Now that you are in recovery, you may want to talk with family members or friends about the disease of addiction and your commitment to recovery. You can start by telling them the following:

- Addiction is a mind, body, spirit disease that causes changes in the brain that can drive a person to use alcohol or other drugs despite negative consequences. For example, while some people can take a drink or two and stop, others can't stop drinking once they start. These people have the disease of addiction.
- Addiction requires a spiritual solution. This means addicts need the help of others, including a Higher Power. Addicts don't have all the answers.
- Recovery is a daily process of living a healthy, balanced life.

Describe the disease of addiction in your own words. Write down the names of supportive family members and friends whom you would like to talk to about addiction.

....

....

....

....

....

....

....

....

"She who conceals her disease cannot expect to be healed."
—Ethiopian Proverb

Practice Serenity

The Serenity Prayer is a cornerstone of Twelve Step recovery: "God, grant me the serenity to accept the things I cannot change, the courage to change the things I can, and the wisdom to know the difference."

In recovery, you learn that serenity is not the absence of conflict or chaos; it is the ability to cope with these things. Life happens, with all its ups and downs, confusion, and joy. Many of these occurrences are outside of your control. The Serenity Prayer asks you to look to your Higher Power for wisdom to let go of the things you cannot change. Learning to live life on life's terms takes some getting used to, which is why it's a good idea to recite this prayer at every meeting and on most days in between. It takes daily practice to let go and let God, but your serenity depends on your ability to do just that.

Write down ten things that are challenging you, then meditate about handing them over to your Higher Power for today.

....

....

....

....

....

....

....

....

"Serenity isn't freedom from the storm; it's peace within it."

Establish a Healthy Sleep Cycle

It's normal to feel sleepless or exhausted in early recovery because withdrawal from alcohol or other drugs can disrupt your sleep patterns. You may have a hard time falling asleep, or you may wake up too early in the morning and not be able to get back to sleep. If you adopt a pattern of poor sleep, you may worry more, which only makes it harder to relax.

You might not be able to establish healthy sleep patterns right away, but eventually you'll get the seven to ten hours of healing sleep the average person needs every night.

If you're having trouble sleeping, describe the thoughts and feelings you notice when you try to go to sleep. If there are things you are obsessing about, try to let go and let God handle your problems, at least for tonight.

_____

_____

_____

_____

_____

_____

_____

_____

_____

_____

*"Have courage for the great sorrows of life
and patience for the small ones; and when you have laboriously accomplished
your daily task, go to sleep in peace."*
—Victor Hugo

Watch Out for Withdrawal

Take a little time each day to monitor how you are feeling emotionally and physically. It's common in early recovery to feel moody, irritable, stressed, clumsy, and impatient and to have trouble concentrating and sleeping. These are normal, temporary symptoms that occur as your body and brain get used to functioning without alcohol or other drugs. These symptoms will go away if you remain sober and continue to work on your recovery. Take care of yourself by making sure you don't get too hungry, angry, lonely, or tired (HALT).

Take a few moments to sit in silence. How does your body feel today? Have you felt tired, overwhelmed, stressed, or sad? Write about anything that comes to mind while you meditate.

....

....

....

....

....

....

....

....

....

....

"The longer I am clean and sober, the clearer my life will become.
I will be patient with myself and give myself time to heal."

Make Room for Healthy Friends

In recovery, loneliness and isolation can be dangerous. The solution is to develop relationships with clean-and-sober friends. When you go to meetings, you'll find a room full of people who understand your situation. They'll listen to you and go for coffee with you afterward. As you see these people week after week, they will become your support network, and you'll have someone to call or see socially when you're lonely or isolated.

Go to a meeting and make a list of the people you think you'd like to connect with. Call one of them this week and make plans to get together outside the meeting.

....

....

....

....

....

....

....

....

....

....

....

"One of the worst things about drinking is the loneliness.
And one of the best things about A.A. is the fellowship."
—*Twenty-Four Hours a Day,* January 30

Create Fun Routines

It may be hard to let go of the crazy parties or nights at the bar that amused you when you were using. Try redefining your idea of fun.

In the past, did you drink at parties every weekend? If so, then start going to a movie with friends every weekend. If you used to go to the bar every Wednesday night, find a coffee shop or bookstore or somewhere else you might like to hang out, and go there every Wednesday night. For every habit you say no to, find something healthy you can say yes to. Use this technique to teach yourself that there are a million ways to enjoy life without drugs.

List your old "fun" routines, and note how it makes you feel to think about them again. Be prepared to call your sponsor or another sober friend if this review ignites any cravings. Describe a few healthy things you can say yes to this week.

....

....

....

....

....

....

....

....

....

....

"A playful path is the shortest road to happiness."

Change Self-Defeating Thoughts and Beliefs

Your thoughts, feelings, and behavior are intertwined. If you think, "I'll never be able to stay sober for the rest of my life," you could become overwhelmed and discouraged, and those feelings might harm your sobriety. If, instead, you think, "I won't worry about the future; I'll focus on staying sober today," you may feel more content and hopeful. These healthier thoughts will lead to actions that support your recovery.

Just as your thoughts can influence feelings and actions, your actions can also influence how you feel and think. If you feel depressed and are thinking discouraging thoughts, get out of the house and go to a meeting. Call a recovery friend or spend time with supportive sober friends and family.

What self-defeating thoughts have you had recently? How can you shift your thinking to be more positive and hopeful? What action could you take to positively influence your thoughts and feelings?

....

....

....

....

....

....

....

....

....

"Fake it till you make it."

Learn How Addiction Happens

Addiction is a serious and progressive disease. You may have tried to quit using, but without drugs in your system, you felt lower than low. Your body became chemically out of balance, and your cravings grew stronger. Your use became worse over time, no doubt, and you built up a tolerance, needing more and more of the drug to get high. After a while, your brain adapted to repeated drug use, overriding your rational thought process. As the disease of addiction began to control you, your life became more and more unmanageable—even when you risked losing everything you value.

Describe a time when you realized you had crossed the line into addiction. Did your addiction cause harsh consequences with family, friends, or employers? Did you suffer financial, legal, or health consequences? Remember, no matter how harsh the consequences, you are capable of healing—like many others before you.

....

....

....

....

....

....

....

....

....

....

"In recovery, we are not bad people becoming good;
we are sick people becoming well."

Interview a Potential Sponsor

You may still be looking for a sponsor who fits your needs. It can be challenging to find someone with whom you can really connect, someone who will hold you accountable for your spiritual growth. Take some time this week to think about a few people who might work.

Once you have identified a potential sponsor, "interview" him or her to see whether your personalities are a good fit. Here are some questions to ask:

- Have you sponsored other people in recovery?
- How do you approach being a sponsor?
- What are the most important things you can help me with as my sponsor?
- What are you doing to actively work your own Twelve Step program?
- What is your experience with spirituality, and how does spirituality help recovery?
- What do you require of me as your sponsee?

Ask any additional questions you have. In a quiet place after the interview, write down what you learned about the potential sponsor.

....

....

....

....

....

....

....

....

"I believe that life is a school in which I must learn spiritual things."
—*Twenty-Four Hours a Day,* February 5

Face Your Fears

It can be scary to face the first few months of life without using alcohol or other drugs. Common fears include returning to substance use, dealing with responsibilities, facing loved ones, encountering the stigma of addiction, going back to work, going to Twelve Step meetings, and not having support. Fortunately, many addicts have used the Steps to face and overcome these fears.

Describe your biggest fears about the next year of recovery. Talk with your sponsor and recovery group about ways to overcome these obstacles.

....

....

....

....

....

....

....

....

....

....

"My Higher Power will not burden me with anything I can't handle.
I pray that I may face every situation without fear because I know
that my Higher Power is at my side."

Stay Focused

Recovery is easier when you stay focused on your reasons for sobriety. You can start by making a list of what you're grateful for—your children, spouse, family, friends, job, home, physical and spiritual health—and read it every day. Use a daily planner or calendar and schedule ten minutes every day for gratitude. Consider this task as high a priority as a business meeting or other appointment.

Write down your reasons for recovery and place reminder notes in locations where you used to drink or use drugs, such as in your bathroom, basement, or car. Take a moment right now to schedule time in your day for gratitude. Write the time down here and in your planner.

"I pray that I can practice gratitude in all things and not forget that all things are given by the grace of God."

Keep Letting Go of Control

One of the most common self-defeating beliefs people have in early recovery is "I know best. I should be in control."

Consider this story from a first-year recovering methamphetamine addict: "In early recovery, I had trouble admitting powerlessness in Step One and Step Two. I'm a strong-willed person, and so I wanted to control my addiction with sheer willpower. It felt humbling to admit that I needed help—even help from a Higher Power. After talking to friends in recovery, I realized that they felt the same way. I realized that letting go also means letting go of shame and guilt. Admitting powerlessness means accepting that I can't control everything in my life, but that I am responsible for the effort I make. There's a certain relief and freedom in letting go of controlling everything and trying to be perfect. I feel more relaxed, serene, and comfortable with myself than I ever have in the past."

Describe your experience with working Step One and Step Two. Do you find ways that they challenge you? Talk to others in your recovery group. It helps to know that others have felt this way. You are not alone.

....

....

....

....

....

....

....

"I pray that I may gladly leave my future in God's hands."
—*Twenty-Four Hours a Day,* June 28

Deal with Emotions

It's normal in early recovery to feel a roller coaster of emotions. In a single day you may experience happiness, grief, anger, gratitude, anxiety, optimism, and depression. The way to handle the ups and downs is to lean on your sponsor, recovery group, and supportive family and friends. Your sponsor and recovery group have experienced what you are going through. They can listen and help guide you through the rough times.

List some things that are bothering you or causing you to feel challenging emotions. Review the list. Are there a few things you can let go of or put aside for now? In your daily life, practice identifying the things you really need to deal with now. Put the other things "on the shelf" until you are stronger.

....

....

....

....

....

....

....

....

....

....

....

"In recovery, I learn how to control my emotions so they don't control me."

Deal with Doubt

Pages 365–366 in *Alcoholics Anonymous* tell us that it's okay, and even natural, to have doubts about the miracle of recovery.

To repel doubt, try to "act as if" you have faith in recovery. This means "trying on" a new belief or a behavior until it becomes more natural. Right now, you may not completely embrace the idea of lifelong recovery. You may be skeptical that sober living will fit your lifestyle. You might doubt that there is a Higher Power that can transform your life. Let go of these doubts and thoughts. Act as if you do have faith in recovery. Go to meetings. Read the Big Book. Listen to and embrace the stories of the people in your recovery group who are living healthy, sober lives. One day—almost without realizing it—you will see that your faith is real and that you are experiencing the life-changing power of recovery.

Describe any doubts you have about recovery. Describe how you might practice "acting as if" as a way to deal with these doubts.

....

....

....

....

....

....

....

....

"It is easier to act yourself into a new way of thinking
than to think yourself into a new way of acting."

Learn to Sleep Naturally

Sleep medications aren't necessarily the solution to sleep problems. Some medications can be addictive. For a natural alternative, try avoiding caffeine after 10:00 a.m. and try not to nap during the day. Save your bedroom for sleeping—avoid the urge to read, write, or watch television in your bedroom. This will help condition your mind that the bedroom equals sleep. You can also try exercising about four hours before bedtime and taking a hot bath right before you go to sleep. Use relaxing rituals, such as meditating or listening to music, before bedtime to help mellow your mind and body.

Don't stay in bed when you have trouble sleeping. Get up and do something relaxing like stretching or meditating, and don't go back to bed until you feel sleepy.

If you are having trouble sleeping, review your thoughts, your activities, and what you've eaten to determine what might be interfering with your sleep. Are you worrying about something from the past or future? What can you do differently tomorrow?

"Sleep is the best meditation."
—His Holiness the Dalai Lama

Combat Loneliness

Early recovery is about change: change in lifestyle, change in relationships, and change within yourself. You might feel lonely because you have cut yourself off from people out of fear or shame. You may be uncertain about what they think of you. Or you might pull back because you aren't ready to make amends to someone you have hurt.

It is important to combat loneliness by surrounding yourself with supportive people. Fortunately, at meetings you will find many people who understand how lonely the first months of recovery can feel. Talk about your feelings at a meeting and find out how other members handle loneliness. Spend time with others by going out to coffee after a meeting, performing volunteer work, or spending time with a sober friend.

List three activities you can do this week that involve connecting with other sober people.

....

....

....

....

....

....

....

....

"Friendship improves happiness and abates misery,
by doubling our joys and dividing our grief."
—Joseph Addison

Take It One Day at a Time

In recovery, you learn that there are two days that should not concern you: yesterday and tomorrow. Once you let go of worrying about the future or bemoaning the past, you discover that today is rich with possibility. You can do many things sober that you may not have been able to do before: write letters, return phone calls, sleep soundly, make love, meditate, play, and be a good parent or friend.

Read what page 345 in *Alcoholics Anonymous* has to say about re-entering the world as a clean-and-sober person. Describe some of the things you enjoy now as you practice living one day at a time without being drunk or high.

....

....

....

....

....

....

....

....

....

"All the money in the world cannot bring back yesterday.
We cannot undo a single act we performed.
We cannot erase a single word we said. Yesterday is gone beyond recall.
Do I still worry about what happened yesterday?"
—*Twenty-Four Hours a Day,* July 29

Set Recovery Goals with Your Family

Your family is not responsible for your recovery, but it may help everyone if you get their assistance and support. Ask supportive family members and friends whether they will help you honor your commitment to attend meetings and communicate with your sponsor. This will increase their understanding and patience about the time you need to devote to your recovery journey. It might help to see a marriage or family counselor if you are having trouble balancing the demands of home life with your necessary recovery activities.

List your ongoing commitments and recovery activities. Describe how your family can support you in these. Write a letter to a supportive family member or friend asking for his or her help. Thank this person in advance.

....

....

....

....

....

....

....

....

....

*"Our true measure of success in life is the measure of spiritual progress
that we have revealed in our lives."*
—*Twenty-Four Hours a Day,* October 29

Let Go of Excuses

You probably invented all sorts of excuses to deny your addiction, justify your behavior, and avoid negative consequences. These excuses can threaten your recovery unless you replace them with the following beliefs: you are powerless against addiction; you have a disease that requires a spiritual solution; and you don't have all the answers. This requires true honesty. Each Step takes you to another level of knowing and accepting yourself. As you refine your self-knowledge, you develop healthier relationships with others.

Read what page 23 in *Alcoholics Anonymous* says about making excuses. Write down some of the excuses you make that impede your recovery. Next to each excuse, list a true statement that supports your recovery and exposes the excuse as a lie. For example:

> *Excuse: "I can't stay in recovery forever. It's too hard."*
> *Truth: "I deserve lifetime recovery. I can have it with the help and guidance of my Higher Power."*

....

....

....

....

....

....

....

....

"Before you say 'I can't,' say 'I'll try.'"

Deal with High-Risk Situations

In early recovery, certain situations threaten your sense of control, making you vulnerable to relapse, including

- negative emotions such as anger, anxiety, depression, frustration, and boredom
- conflict with friends, co-workers, or family
- being around others who are drinking or using
- celebrations or emotional events
- exposure to alcohol or other drug-related stimuli, such as certain advertisements
- attempts to use "just a little"

Identify your high-risk situations, and work with your sponsor to create a plan to deal with them. You can't avoid all high-risk situations, but you can develop healthy responses such as leaving a "sticky" situation, practicing positive affirmations, or contacting a sober friend.

Make a list of high-risk situations that could trigger a relapse, and pair each with a coping strategy. Then make plans to practice new skills and thinking in order to keep your life in balance.

....

....

....

....

....

....

"Even after ten years of recovery, I know I can't afford to become complacent.
Attending Twelve Step meetings helps me handle any triggers
or high-risk situations that could cause me to relapse."

Learn to Lighten Up

Recovery is hard work, but a sense of humor can help you lighten up when things go wrong. One way to keep your sense of humor is to let go and laugh. Remind yourself often that you aren't in control and things sometimes just don't turn out the way you think they should.

List some of the simple things that went wrong this week that were outside of your control. Maybe your car wouldn't start or your child spilled ice cream all over your new sofa. Can you laugh about the situation? Will these little problems matter a year from now? Try to laugh and lighten your load.

....

....

....

....

....

....

....

....

....

....

....

....

"Laughter is the sun that drives winter from the human face."
—Victor Hugo

Practice Positive Affirmations

Affirmations are empowering statements about the ways you want to think, feel, and behave. They help you feel deserving and confident instead of guilt-ridden and shameful. Affirmations are not a substitute for reality; they are a way to tap into your best self, the inner strength that may have been overshadowed in the grips of addiction.

In the early stages of recovery, you spend a lot of time focusing on changing negative patterns of compulsion, denial, and self-destructive behavior. Affirmations are a way to assert that you are ready to celebrate your best self right now.

Start by paying attention to your negative attitudes and self-talk. Write down those dark messages on a separate piece of paper and throw them away. Replace the negatives with positives such as "I am a good and loving person." Read these out loud. Celebrate yourself! Describe all the good things you have to offer.

....

....

....

....

....

....

....

....

....

"Negativity is my disease asking me to come out and play."

Practice True Faith

Step Two: "Came to believe that a Power greater than ourselves could restore us to sanity."

Because of their illness, addicts often put their faith in the wrong things, such as drugs, alcohol, using friends, or their own addicted mind. Many try to "play God" during their using days. They believe they have the ultimate plan for themselves and for others. They are always right. They try to make others conform to their own ideas of how the world should be. Their quest for control may have crushed any spiritual nature they had.

When you searched for happiness during your active addiction, you found a void in your life. You may have tried to fill that void with drugs, money, relationships, material things, or compulsive behaviors, but these didn't resolve your internal needs. What you really need is to seek the spirituality that will give your life meaning.

Read page 25 in *Alcoholics Anonymous*. Describe a few of the unhealthy things you used to fill your spiritual void. Think about ways you can start to let go of controlling yourself and others. Can you start to hand over a few of your worries to your Higher Power?

....

....

....

....

....

....

....

....

"How do you know if you've got Step Two? You have a sliver of hope."

Develop Supportive Friendships

Sobriety isn't something you can do in isolation. You need friends to help you do what you can't do alone. Friends used to be the people you borrowed money from or called when you wanted to go out drinking. Your sober friends will be the people who listen when you need to talk. They'll understand your problems because they've had the same kinds of problems themselves. They'll answer the phone when you call. They'll give you the guidance you need when you encounter a problem you can't solve. They'll include you in activities that don't involve alcohol or other drugs.

Read page 276 in *Alcoholics Anonymous*. Write down all the ways that friends have helped you so far. If there's something you need that you haven't asked a friend for, ask yourself why you haven't.

....

....

....

....

....

....

....

....

....

"A true friend knows your weaknesses but shows you your strengths;
feels your fears but fortifies your faith; sees your anxieties but frees your spirit;
recognizes your disabilities but emphasizes your possibilities."
—William Arthur Ward

Learn More about Relapse

What exactly is a relapse? People often think of a relapse as one event, such as the first time they break sobriety by drinking a beer or snorting cocaine. But relapse is really the chain of events that happens when a person becomes unable to cope with life in sobriety. Not all recovering people relapse, but many do have brief relapse episodes before they achieve long-term abstinence.

You may be at risk of relapse if you engage in high-risk situations, fail to practice the Steps, lack coping skills, or try to control your drug use on your own. These warning signs happen long before you take that first drink. If you are aware of the warning signs, you'll be able to get help before you end up with a drink in your hand.

Are you at risk? List any warning signs you are experiencing. Talk these over with your sponsor or recovery group.

....

....

....

....

....

....

....

....

....

....

"It's not what happens to you, but how you react to it that matters."
—Epictetus

Connect with Your Sponsor

Will Rogers once said, "You might be on the right track, but you'll still get run over if you just sit there." To keep moving forward, make sure you connect with your sponsor and your recovery group. Research shows that people who participate in a Twelve Step group have much better short- and long-term recovery rates than people who don't. This is because Twelve Step groups provide the acceptance, structure, and stability you need to learn and practice the new life skills that are essential to recovery.

Are you attending meetings and talking with your sponsor at least once a week? Are you talking about your issues at meetings? Do you socialize with group members? Do you read the Big Book? If not, describe what's holding you back. Make a commitment to see your sponsor and attend at least one meeting this week. Reach out to at least one member with whom you would like a deeper connection.

....

....

....

....

....

....

....

....

"YANA = You Are Not Alone"

Congratulations for working on Step Two! You are beginning to heal your mind, body, and spirit. If you notice your old ways and thoughts resurfacing, go back and review the lessons you learned in this Step.

Surrender in Order to Grow

DAY 66 TO DAY 95

Trust Your Higher Power

Step Three: "Made a decision to turn our will and our lives over to the care of God *as we understood Him.*"

In Step One, you admitted powerlessness. In Step Two, you acknowledged the need for a Higher Power and that spirituality holds the key to true recovery. In Step Three, you're ready to take action by getting out of your Higher Power's way and trusting that this force can guide you to make healthy choices. Step Three asks you to stop trying to take charge. In exchange, you will worry less and trust more.

This act of surrender takes courage and practice. It is like learning to float in water. When you stop thrashing about and begin to relax and lie back, you discover that the water will hold you.

Read the prayer on page 63 in *Alcoholics Anonymous.* Describe how you can trust your Higher Power and be relieved of "the bondage of self."

....

....

....

....

....

....

....

....

....

....

"Let go and let God."

Understand Addictive Thinking

"I'll have just one drink, then I'll stop." "I don't want to hang out with all those losers at NA. I'm sick of people trying to run my life." These statements are examples of addictive thinking, or "stinking thinking": denials or justifications used to defend or rationalize your drug use.

Work to replace stinking thinking with the basic lessons of the Steps. When you catch yourself wanting to have "just one drink" or hang out with a using friend, say these two recovery affirmations out loud:

1. I am powerless against addiction, so I must not use any mood-altering substances. Not ever.
2. I have the disease of addiction. The solution is spiritual, which means I can't recover alone. I trust my Higher Power to guide me.

Describe three examples of your own stinking thinking, and write an affirmation in response to each addictive thought. Here's an example:

> *Stinking thinking: I can have just one drink and stop.*
> *Affirmation: I cannot control my use of any mood-altering substances.*
> *Not ever.*

....

....

....

....

"If we allow an alcoholic thought to lodge in our minds . . . we are in danger
of having a slip. Therefore we must dispel such thoughts at once . . .
by immediately putting constructive thoughts in their place."
—*Twenty-Four Hours a Day,* December 4

Review Your Relapse Warning Signs

Read what pages 396–397 in *Alcoholics Anonymous* say about relapse. Review your relapse warning signs and high-risk situations. Ask yourself whether you are hungry, angry, lonely, or tired (HALT).

Review your relapse response plan or create a new plan if you haven't developed one yet. Give copies to your sponsor and others who support your recovery so they will know what to do to help you. The plan should include

- the people or places you can call for help (sponsor, supportive family member or friend, treatment center)
- the places you can go for help (meetings, sponsor's house, treatment center, physician's office)
- thoughts that will motivate you to prevent relapse (loss of family, friends, career, or health)
- a "last resort" contract such as "if I am unwilling to follow this plan, I agree to check into a treatment center"

....

....

....

....

....

....

....

*"We have to learn to think straight . . . to change from alcoholic thinking
to sober thinking . . . We must reeducate our minds."*
—*Twenty-Four Hours a Day,* January 21

Practice Taking Life in Small Steps

"Today I will do one thing." Use this slogan to remind you that your task is to take life one small step at a time. Don't allow yourself to start worrying about tomorrow, next week, or next month. Don't become impatient. Change happens day by day, not overnight. Give yourself credit for the small steps you take every day to work on your recovery.

At this point in recovery, you may notice that you are being more honest with others and more open and willing to put your recovery and spirituality ahead of everything else in your life. List some of the small daily changes you have made that benefit your recovery. Give yourself a lot of credit for these small steps. Every small step helps you build healthy routines that move you forward in recovery.

....

....

....

....

....

....

....

....

....

....

"Faith, positive thinking, and patience can move mountains.
I pray that I may be more accepting of myself and others,
and trust and rely more on my Higher Power for guidance."

Keep Letting Go of Control

Recovery has been described as the balance between letting it happen and making it happen. *Alcoholics Anonymous* talks about the link between addiction and the need to control on pages 60–61, comparing the addict to an actor who wants to be in charge of the entire show: the lights, the stage set, and the other actors. However, the best actors know the importance of a good director. They trust in the director's expertise and know if they only follow directions, the director will bring out the best in them. Your Higher Power is the director of the drama called life.

Write down five things you've attempted to control recently. What is preventing you from handing these over to your Higher Power?

....

....

....

....

....

....

....

....

....

....

"Just for today, I will adjust myself to what is,
and not try to adjust everything else to my desires."

Practice Prayer and Meditation

Prayer and meditation are ways to communicate with your Higher Power. Some recovering people say that prayer is talking to your Higher Power, while meditation is listening to your Higher Power.

You may want to set aside a certain time (first thing in the morning or after dinner, for example) for some silence or time to pray to your Higher Power. You might start communicating by writing a letter to your Higher Power. Share any fears you have about recovery. Ask for guidance or direction, or just talk about how you feel today.

Start writing your letter here. Read your letter out loud, then take a few minutes to sit in silence. Meditate by being still and listening for guidance.

....

....

....

....

....

....

....

....

....

....

"My Higher Power is always with me—I just need to be still and listen."

Improve Relationships

It's important to have people you can ask for help when you need it. You have probably completed your list of people you can count on for support. These people are very important in your life. Take some time to check in on these relationships.

Write down the names of at least three people who are very important in supporting your recovery. For example, you might list your spouse or significant other. You might list your sponsor, a sober friend, or a supportive family member. Ask yourself these questions and write your answers next to each person's name:

1. Are you being honest and open with this person?
2. Are you holding resentments against this person?
3. How can you be more accepting in this relationship?
4. How can you focus more on the positive?
5. How can you be less controlling with this person?
6. Are your expectations of this person reasonable?

....

....

....

....

....

....

....

....

"You can't shake hands with a clenched fist."
—Indira Gandhi

Identify Emotions

It is important to acknowledge the range of emotions you experience, but those emotions don't need to rule your life. Remember that all emotions pass eventually. You are not your emotions. You exist regardless of the temporary and fleeting emotions that you experience today.

Addicts know all about using drugs to mask pain, feel pleasure, or lower inhibitions. If you feel too much or too little, you may be tempted to use alcohol or other drugs in an attempt to control the way you feel. Using drugs to control your feelings only creates a vicious cycle that feeds on itself. You feel bad, you use drugs. You may feel a short-term high, but then your emotions will drop into despair, and you will need to use more drugs just to feel relaxed and "normal."

Being comfortable with challenging feelings is not easy for anyone. It's especially hard if you have denied, ignored, hid from, or lied about them for years. It helps to describe the way you feel by writing in your journal each day.

Describe the last time you felt anxious, peaceful, excited, or tired—and note when you began to feel differently. With whom can you share this exercise (giving that person equal time to also discuss his or her feelings)?

....

....

....

....

....

....

"Alcoholic emotions may either make or break us.
It seems necessary that we learn their constructive use."
—*The Little Red Book*

Take Care of Your Body

Abusing drugs upsets your body's natural balance in different ways. You may have lost weight and become malnourished due to stimulant use or gained weight because you felt depressed from alcohol use. You also may have become dehydrated or let go of personal hygiene because you stayed awake for days while binging on methamphetamine or other drugs.

Take a moment to thank your Higher Power that you're no longer actively damaging your body with alcohol or other drugs. Write down your drug of choice, and reflect on what was probably happening to your body while you were using.

....

....

....

....

....

....

....

....

....

....

....

"In recovery, the life you save is your own."

Improve Your Spirituality

The prayer on page 63 in *Alcoholics Anonymous* teaches you that your Higher Power is in charge. Your Higher Power is the instructor and you are the student. Prayer and meditation deepen your relationship with your Higher Power and help you overcome self-will. Prayer is talking to your Higher Power, and meditation is listening to your Higher Power. You can pray for courage and for relief from anger, fear, and grief. You can meditate to clear your mind and restore calm. Whatever the prayer or meditation, remember to interact with your Higher Power every day.

Re-read the Big Book prayer on page 63. Take a few minutes to write this prayer using your own words. Keep it in a place where you can read it every day.

....

....

....

....

....

....

....

....

....

*"Grace is available for each of us every day—our spiritual daily bread—
but we've got to remember to ask for it with a grateful heart
and not worry about whether there will be enough for tomorrow."*
—Sarah Ban Breathnach

Recognize Self-Pity

It is normal to feel sorry for yourself from time to time. You might feel that addiction has stripped all the good things from your life, and you may feel a lot of self-pity as a result. But self-pity makes recovery even more difficult. You can't build a positive life in the present if you can't let go of the past.

When you focus your attention on the present, you take back your power. You don't have to blame anyone or anything else for your addiction or for situations that caused you pain. This week, focus on letting go of the past and start to focus on what you can do today to feel better and protect your sobriety. Your Higher Power has a plan for you that is greater than any pain in your past.

Read page 8 in *Alcoholics Anonymous,* and see what it says about self-pity. Describe the last time you remember feeling sorry for yourself. Make a commitment to take your power back by focusing on the present and letting go of what happened in the past. The past is over. The future is now.

....

....

....

....

....

....

....

"Finish each day and be done with it. You have done what you could.
Some blunders and absurdities no doubt crept in; forget them
as soon as you can. Tomorrow is a new day; begin it well and serenely
and with too high a spirit to be encumbered with your old nonsense."
—Ralph Waldo Emerson

Use Affirmations for Growth and Change

Affirmations replace unhealthy messages with positive ones. Repeating positive affirmations as if you're already accomplishing them improves your attitude, and as your attitude changes, so does your life. Affirmations like these will strengthen your willingness to change your life:

- I surrender my will and life to my Higher Power.
- I learn from others.
- I let others live their lives.
- I laugh and allow myself to enjoy life.
- I say "I'm sorry" when I'm wrong.

Make a commitment to write your own affirmations on index cards. Remember to write them in the present tense, not the future tense (for example, "I surrender" instead of "I will surrender"). Carry the cards with you to read during difficult times.

....

....

....

....

....

....

....

....

"Change your thoughts and you change your world."
—Norman Vincent Peale

Sleep Well

You may be discovering that even sleep is better sober. You aren't waking up with hangovers, and you don't have to worry about what you did or didn't do the night before. You may even be waking up feeling hopeful and content after a good night's sleep. This happens when you're getting the kind of sleep that allows for psychological healing and physical repair.

Reflect on how your sleep has changed since you quit using drugs. Is your sleep quality improving? Are you dreaming less than you did when you first got sober? Do you feel better after sleeping than you used to? Write down the answers to these questions. Talk to your sponsor if you are still having difficulty sleeping.

....

....

....

....

....

....

....

....

....

"Finish each day before you begin the next, and interpose a solid wall of sleep between the two. This you cannot do without temperance."
—Ralph Waldo Emerson

Deal with Triggers

Triggers can be emotions or memories that cause you to crave alcohol or other drugs. You've probably heard a song on the radio that reminded you of your first date and brought back nostalgic memories of youth. The smell of warm cookies may trigger memories of Grandma's house and of warmth and safety. Triggers work the same way. Many addicts salivate when they see a chilled beer in a TV commercial, or they have intense cravings while watching drug scenes in a movie. This is normal but should be avoided because it can cause you to relapse.

What are your triggers? Discuss them with your sponsor and develop a plan to avoid anything that may cause you to relapse.

....

....

....

....

....

....

....

....

....

*"We should never forget physical drunkenness is always preceded
by mental binges that end in spiritual blackouts."*
—*The Little Red Book*

Enjoy the Beauty of Life

Are you starting to incorporate sober fun into your daily life? It helps to think about what you're feeling, and what kind of fun might best accompany that feeling. If you're feeling curious, it might be fun to try something new, such as a class, volunteer opportunity, or museum visit. If you're feeling restless and energetic, put that energy to use during a hike, walk, run, or bicycle ride. Offer to help someone else, or clean your house while listening to your favorite music.

If you're feeling tense or sad, try meeting a friend whose company you really enjoy. Or, if you'd rather stay home and be quiet, take a warm bath. You'll soon discover that the beauty of life is all around you. If you think you can't enjoy your life without getting high, recognize that this is your addiction talking. Talk about these thoughts with your sponsor.

Describe the ways you have experienced the beauty of life in the last week. How is your experience of life different than when you were using alcohol and other drugs?

....

....

....

....

....

....

....

....

....

"Smile every day. Recovery is serious business, but don't forget to have fun."

Understand Depression and Addiction

It's hard to tell sometimes whether you're actually depressed or just feeling the ordinary turmoil of addiction. It may be difficult—even a little depressing—to let go of drugs and face the emotions that your addiction cushioned you from. Feeling lots of emotional ups and downs is normal in early recovery. Depression, however, has some general symptoms, including

- ongoing sadness, hopelessness, guilt, and feelings of worthlessness or helplessness
- loss of interest in hobbies or normal activities
- ongoing fatigue, restlessness, or irritability
- difficulty concentrating or making decisions
- insomnia or oversleeping
- changes in appetite or weight
- persistent headaches, digestive disorders, or chronic pain
- thoughts of suicide

Have you experienced any of these symptoms? How have they affected your life, relationships, and thinking? Talk to your sponsor about these experiences. If you feel down and you suspect that your depression is more than a temporary feeling, ask your sponsor to help you get an assessment from a mental health professional as soon as possible.

....

....

....

....

....

....

*"It was a blessed relief when I accepted depression
as another disease I can treat, but not control."*

Practice Prayer

Prayer is as simple as taking time to talk and connect with your Higher Power. If prayer is new to you, keep it simple. The first step is to imagine a Higher Power, whether it's God, the universe, the spirit of nature, or a benevolent friend. The second step is to focus your prayer. Think about the challenges you face. Ask your Higher Power for help. Think about recent successes and growth you have experienced. Thank your Higher Power for making it possible. Remember that prayer does not involve asking your Higher Power to give you everything you want or desire. Instead, it's a chance to ask for divine guidance because you don't know it all. You don't have all the answers.

Follow the directions above and write a simple prayer in your own words. Take the time to practice the prayer in a quiet place that is free from distraction.

....

....

....

....

....

....

....

....

....

....

"Prayer does not change God, but it changes [the person] who prays."
—Søren Kiekegaard

Remedy Doubt

In your first weeks of recovery, you may have questioned your faith in your Higher Power, your trust in your sponsor, or the value of the Steps. Months into recovery, you may still have occasional doubts about whether you can maintain sobriety and eventually achieve the serenity promised in Twelve Step recovery. Such doubts are normal. They don't mean you are doing something wrong or "flunking" recovery.

Practicing recovery is like getting used to a stiff pair of jeans. You try on new ideas and behaviors and wear them each day until they fit better. With time, patience, and practice, you will be able to move more naturally as you become comfortable with your recovery program.

One way to remedy doubt is to write a positive affirmation for each doubt that arises. If you wonder about your sponsor's advice, for example, try writing something like "I trust in my sponsor's knowledge of and experience with the Twelve Steps."

"Modest doubt is called the beacon of the wise."
—William Shakespeare

Meditate to Relieve Loneliness

In your using days, you probably felt isolated or lonely and used drugs to try to fit in. In all likelihood, the loneliness was still there when the drugs wore off.

Now that you're sober, you might still feel lonely, especially if your using friends were your only friends. But feeling lonely is only temporary, and you'll soon move to a healthier, more supportive network of friends.

Meditation is one way to handle challenging emotions like loneliness. Focus on your breathing and try to clear your mind of your racing thoughts. Let go of your fears and need for control and center yourself. If you lose your sense of relaxation and start to obsess about your feelings, just focus on your breathing again and bring yourself back. With practice, you'll be able to clear your mind of the challenging feelings that may be overtaking you.

Try meditating for ten minutes today, and refocus on your breathing as often as you need to. Listen to your Higher Power, and ask for guidance in dealing with any challenging feelings that arise.

....

....

....

....

....

....

....

....

"When you walk with your Higher Power, you never walk alone."

Acclimate to the Workplace

If you have returned to work after an extended absence, you may suspect that co-workers are aware of your addiction, and you may worry whether they'll judge you. The stigma about addiction exists, and you can't predict how people will react. Many don't understand addiction and may be shocked to learn what you've been through. Those who have been hurt by chemical dependency might not want to hear about it. Others might be very supportive. Talk to your sponsor and recovery group before you decide which co-workers (if any) to confide in.

If you think returning to work full time might jeopardize your recovery, you may want to see whether it is possible to start out on a reduced schedule. Protect your recovery by avoiding triggers, going to meetings, talking to others in recovery who have re-entered the workplace, and being selective about whom you tell.

Describe how you feel about being back at work. Which co-workers do you think support you? Share your feelings with your recovery support group and your sponsor.

....

....

....

....

....

....

....

*"Today try to be stronger, braver, more loving
as a result of what you did yesterday."*
—*Twenty-Four Hours a Day,* September 5

Keep Strengthening Courage

Little children often imagine monsters under the bed, outside the window, or in the closet. In time, they learn that it was just the wind making noises or the moonlight creating a harmless shadow on the wall. The older they get, the braver they become. In much the same way, your fears will begin to dissipate as you grow in a spiritual, sober life. As time passes and your experience grows, you will be able to face your fears about the future, the past, changing relationships, and a life without alcohol or other drug use.

Describe how your fears have evolved, changed, or diminished now that you have been in recovery for several months. Is it getting easier?

....

....

....

....

....

....

....

....

....

....

"[Courage is] a quality of mind which enables us to deal with
the problems and realities of life without reliance on alcohol."
—*The Little Red Book*

Connect at Meetings

After a couple of weeks of meetings and conscious participation in fellowship, you may find that you're feeling greater trust in others. People may have reached out to you after meetings to talk about their experiences or their gratitude for the fellowship of recovery. Or they may invite you to coffee afterward just to chat. Try accepting some of these invitations and see what happens.

Do you see yourself trusting others more as a result of your willingness to connect with them? Describe some ways you've reached out to others this week.

....

....

....

....

....

....

....

....

....

....

....

"I pray that I may be helped and healed by true spiritual fellowship."
—*Twenty-Four Hours a Day,* March 8

Plan for Celebrations and Holidays

Holidays and celebrations can be great times, but they can also be emotional and stressful, which can threaten your sobriety. If you are traveling away from your own home, you may have a lot of unstructured free time with little or no access to your sponsor or recovery support group. And there may be alcohol or drugs present at the celebration.

You can decline invitations (even from family) if any event threatens your sobriety. Your sponsor can help you plan for possible triggers. If you can, take along a friend in recovery. Make sure you plan a ride home in advance—just in case you need to leave suddenly because your sobriety is threatened.

List some upcoming events you want to attend, and detail a few strategies to protect your sobriety while you are there.

....

....

....

....

....

....

....

....

....

*"My friend and I planned to go to a party where there would be an open bar.
I wasn't sure how I would react, so we decided we'd drive separately.
I brought another recovering person with me to the party,
plus the phone number of my sponsor in case I needed extra support."*

Keep Using the Big Book

There is a joke in recovery groups that if you want to hide something from a Twelve Step member, put it in the Big Book. Have you ever read something once and declared yourself "finished" with it? You are never finished with recovery because addiction is an ongoing disease. Unless you continue to work the Steps and practice recovery, you risk relapse.

Alcoholics Anonymous, also called the Big Book, is a trusted companion that guides you through the ups and downs of recovery. Although you change as you grow in recovery, the Big Book remains constant, always ready to comfort and counsel. Revisit the Big Book whenever you need inspiration. Remember, it has offered spiritual guidance and hope to millions of people for decades. Depending on where you are in working the Twelve Steps, you might want to look up Big Book topics on spirituality, forgiveness, or making amends.

Look up an issue that pertains to you today. Describe in your own words what the Big Book has to say about that topic.

....

....

....

....

....

....

....

....

"Keep coming back. It works if you work it."

Keep Working Step Three

Your favorite mentors were probably patient and compassionate people who offered gentle guidance without judgment. Some recovering people worry that they become weak and overly dependent if they turn their lives over to a Higher Power, but this isn't the case. When you turn your will over to a benevolent Higher Power, you are not diminished. Your Higher Power contains unlimited forgiveness and unconditional acceptance, and you are made stronger.

The slogan "Let go and let God" is a reminder that you do not walk alone or unaided on the path of recovery. Some people might say "Trust the universe." A writer with writers' block might be told to "Trust the process." No matter how you put it, these sayings help you realize that the harder you try to control a behavior, a person, or a creative endeavor, the less likely you are to succeed.

Describe in your own words what success in recovery means to you. How does turning your will over to your Higher Power help you achieve it?

....

....

....

....

....

....

....

....

....

"Success is not getting what you want; it's knowing what you don't need."

Give Up the Need to Control

Most addicts have an almost obsessive need to control circumstances and people because they have no control over their addiction. Letting go of your need to control frees you to appreciate the wonderful surprises each day holds. You become more spontaneous and accepting. The rain that canceled your picnic lets you snuggle in and read. A difficult situation at work beyond your control lets you bond with a co-worker.

Write down your answers to the following questions and discuss them with your sponsor or Twelve Step group:

- How do you feel when people don't want to do it your way?
- Do you compulsively control even little things, such as how pictures are hung or how items are arranged in a desk drawer?
- How comfortable are you letting someone else be in charge?
- Are you willing to listen to another viewpoint before sharing yours?
- Are you compelled to correct others' mistakes?
- Is it difficult for you to ask for help?

"If you want to make God laugh, just tell him your plans."
—Jewish Proverb

Be Generous

In early recovery, it's appropriate to focus on yourself. You are starting to recognize the attitudes, thoughts, and behaviors that you need to change in order to stay sober. As you continue in recovery, however, you must practice getting outside of yourself by helping someone each day. Your generosity can be a very small thing, like holding the door for someone or letting another driver merge easily into your lane. If you see new people in meetings who are struggling, be kind. Offer to make them a cup of coffee or introduce them to other group members.

Make a commitment to do something nice for another person this week. Describe how you might help someone else out.

....

....

....

....

....

....

....

....

....

....

*"Helping others is one of the best ways to stay sober yourself.
And the satisfaction you get out of helping a fellow human being
is one of the finest experiences you can have."*
—*Twenty-Four Hours a Day,* May 20

Meditate to Be Free

Find a quiet spot where you can rest without distraction. Read the August 23 meditation from the book *Twenty-Four Hours a Day*: "Keep in mind the goal you are striving for, the good life you are trying to attain. Do not let little things divert you from the path. Do not be overcome by the small trials and vexations of each day. Try to see the purpose and plan to which all is leading. If, when climbing a mountain, you keep your eyes on each stony or difficult place, you grow weary. But if you think of each step as leading to the summit of achievement from which a glorious landscape will open out before you, then your climb will be endurable and you will achieve your goal."

Describe how you feel about this meditation. Are there little things that get in the way of your recovery work? Do you work too much or focus on negative experiences from the past? Be quiet and listen. The answers will come to you.

....

....

....

....

....

....

....

....

"Compassion for others begins with kindness to ourselves."
—Pema Chödrön

Surrender Your Willfulness

It is no easy task to turn your will and your life over to the care of your Higher Power, as Step Three advises. In the stranglehold of addiction, your will is self-defeating and blocks your spirituality. If you could will yourself sober, you would have done it long ago. Addiction clouds your thinking, and in early recovery, you discover you are not the best judge of yourself. Surrendering your willfulness means that you need to look to others—your sponsor, your recovery group, or your Higher Power—to help you stay on the road to recovery. Trust that they have your best interests at heart, and practice asking them for guidance.

Is there a friend or activity you want to pursue? A place you think you want to visit? Write down three decisions you need to make, then list the people you trust to help you make them.

....

....

....

....

....

....

....

....

....

....

....

"When you find yourself in a hole, stop digging."

Stay on Track

Once you accept that you have the disease of addiction, you know that you can't predict how you will react when you are around alcohol or other drugs. To stay on track, you will need to form daily routines that keep you away from people, places, and things that could cause you to crave drugs. Each day try to

- start the day with a reading from the Big Book or a meditation book
- talk to at least one person in recovery whom you admire (preferably by going to a meeting)
- spend time with family members and sober friends
- take time to offer gratitude for today
- end the day with a few minutes of silence to be open to the direction of your Higher Power

Think about ways you can improve your daily routine in order to stay on track. Describe some positive habits you can start practicing.

....

....

....

....

....

....

"Why are we Masters of our Fate, the captains of our souls?
Because we have the power to control our thoughts, our attitudes.
That is why many people live in the withering negative world.
That is why many people live in the Positive Faith world.
And you don't have to be a poet or a philosopher to know which is best."
—Alfred A. Montapert

Congratulations for working on Step Three! You are beginning to surrender in order to grow. If you notice your old ways and thoughts resurfacing, go back and review the lessons you learned in this Step.

Be Fearless

DAY 96 TO DAY 125

Perform a Moral Inventory

Step Four: "Made a searching and fearless moral inventory of ourselves."

Conducting a moral inventory helps you get to know and love yourself more deeply. For many addicts, addiction negatively affected the people they love. Step Four offers a way for you to take responsibility and then let go of any shame and guilt you are holding on to from the past.

For those addicts who were abused, Step Four helps them deal with feelings of anger, fear, and resentment toward others. Step Four encourages them to see that it is people's actions, not the people themselves, that are bad. If you can forgive yourself, then you can also learn to forgive others.

Don't let the past continue to control you. Read what pages 64–71 in *Alcoholics Anonymous* say about Step Four. When you take a close look at how your actions have harmed others, you give yourself the gift of honesty. Describe how it feels to begin this process. How will it feel to be free from guilt and regret about the past?

....

....

....

....

....

....

....

....

....

"Step Four allowed me to live with myself."

Perform a Resentment Inventory

Start Step Four by performing a resentment inventory. A resentment is unresolved anger that keeps you stuck at the point of pain. It's the opposite of forgiveness. You may be angry with someone who isn't in your life anymore, such as a former supervisor or a parent who has died. You may feel rage toward someone who doesn't understand how you feel or know why you are angry. In the end, you are the only one who suffers from holding on to resentment. Follow these steps to perform a resentment inventory:

1. List any people or situations that you resent.
2. What is the cause of each of these resentments? What happened?
3. Where were you to blame? What could you have done to deal with the situation in a healthy way?

Make a commitment to share your resentment inventory with your sponsor.

"If we give out hate, we will become hateful. If we are resentful,
we will be resented. If we do not like people, we will not be liked by people."
—*Twenty-Four Hours a Day,* November 7

Trust the Process

Now that you are working Step Four, you are faced with the difficult and often painful task of reviewing the harms you have caused others. This can be a challenging process of self-discovery. So, while you work this Step, be sure to take some time to lighten up and enjoy life. Working the Steps may feel hard right now, but trust that you will feel more joy and peace as you connect with your Higher Power and enrich your relationships with others. Keep reminding yourself that you are worth the work.

Review your week and write down all the moments of joy and peace you can recall. What made you smile or laugh? Practice smiling more, and notice when more joy begins to come your way.

....

....

....

....

....

....

....

....

....

....

....

"Joy is an inside job."

Watch Out for Stinking Thinking

"I'll have just one drink, then I'll stop." "Meetings are for people who are weak. I'm different. I don't need help. I'm fine on my own." In early recovery, you might have engaged in "stinking thinking" like this in order to exert control—and to avoid relying on your Higher Power or others for help. As you gain more wisdom in recovery, you will begin to spot stinking thinking right away because you will see it as flawed and dishonest. But stay aware because stinking thinking can creep back into your consciousness in subtle ways that you might not notice at first. For example, you might catch yourself thinking, "If others had this many problems, they'd use too."

Remember that the Big Book calls addictive substances "cunning, baffling, powerful." It takes diligence and honest work to overcome that stranglehold. To avoid addictive thinking, you need to stay aware on a daily basis. If you make an honest evaluation of your thinking, you may find some lies, denial, and rationalization. This requires extreme self-honesty.

Make a list of your stinking thinking from the past week. Describe what you could do to spot stinking thinking more quickly. Make a commitment to yourself to stay drug-free.

....

....

....

....

....

....

....

....

"I will not let a cunning chemical take control of my life."

Avoid a Relapse

You already know that relapse is much more than simply taking a drink or using a drug after a period of abstinence. It is a process that starts with predictable warning signs that escalate before that first slip occurs.

Just being aware of how relapse happens is not enough. Each and every day you need to avoid the situations and thinking that could put you in a vulnerable situation. In early recovery, it's likely that your stress levels are high. You are experiencing intense emotional and physical changes, and you are just starting to practice reliable coping skills. Plus, your brain may still be clouded by years of drug use. Or you may be feeling overly confident and deny that you have to deal with the chronic, lifelong disease of addiction. You may start to think you have some control over your drug use. This thinking could cause you to place yourself in high-risk situations where you are likely to end up using.

Take a minute and describe your thoughts and fears about relapse. If you relapse, will you call your sponsor immediately? Make that commitment today.

....

....

....

....

....

....

....

....

....

"Relapse and recovery are processes, not events."

Restore Balance

Your body produces brain chemicals that help control your mood, sleeping patterns, and appetite. Alcohol and other drugs affect your brain chemistry in negative ways. The good news is that your body and mind can heal quickly if you give them what they need. If you quit using all drugs, get eight to ten hours of sleep a night, eat a balanced diet, and engage in regular aerobic exercise, you can help rebalance your brain chemistry. Exercise also reduces stress, decreases depression, and restores self-esteem.

Your body doesn't care what activity you choose, just as long as you keep it moving. Take the stairs, do yoga, go for a walk, ride a bike, join a gym. Remember to check with your doctor before beginning any exercise program.

List some things you could do to get your body moving this week.

....

....

....

....

....

....

....

....

....

....

"The only exercise some of us get is jumping to conclusions."

Reach Out

In the past, you may have avoided asking for help or talking about your problems because you thought it signaled weakness. The truth is that it shows great strength and wisdom to seek mentorship and help from others. The power of going to meetings is in receiving guidance from your fellow addicts and giving help in return. If you attend meetings regularly, you will find that they are a safe place where you can be yourself. Remember that others in the room have been in your shoes. They've found a place to belong, and you can too.

Go to a meeting this week and look around at your fellow addicts. Think of them as having the same fears as you.

Describe some of your biggest fears and challenges. At the next meeting you attend, let go of your pride and share at least one of your fears with the group.

....

....

....

....

....

....

....

....

"A hermit's life is not a normal or natural one . . .
we cannot really live without the companionship of others . . .
Do I fully appreciate what the fellowship of A.A. means to me?"
—*Twenty-Four Hours a Day,* December 9

Avoid Triggers

Triggers include any experience that could lead you to take that first drink or hit. Right now you are probably pretty good at avoiding obvious triggers that could lead to a quick return to drug use. You know to avoid driving by a liquor store on the way home, going to bars, or hanging out with your old using friends. Those are obvious triggers. But you also need to avoid the subtle triggers that are just as dangerous to your sobriety.

For now, try your best to avoid any situation that will cause you a lot of stress. For example, this might not be the best time to try to make up with an old boyfriend or girlfriend. But some things can't be avoided or put off. You may be confronted with unforeseen challenges such as the loss of a spouse or significant other, a job, or a friend.

If you feel like you want to use, call your sponsor immediately. Go to a meeting as soon as possible. Your recovery support network will help you make it through the moment, then the next, until the trigger passes.

What triggers have you experienced this week? Describe how you felt and what you did to deal with them. Whom will you call when you feel tempted to drink, get high, or use any mood-altering substance?

....

....

....

....

....

....

....

"My Higher Power is my shield. The problems of the world cannot truly harm me. Nothing in this world has the power to spoil my inward peace."
—Adapted from *Twenty-Four Hours a Day,* July 28

Learn from Letting Go of Resentments

In Latin, the word "resent" means "to feel again." It is crucial that you realize that there is no upside to resentment. It is a destructive emotion that keeps you from accessing your Higher Power. Keeping hurts alive will inhibit your growth in other relationships as well, and it can lead to their ultimate destruction.

Once you've completed your resentment inventory, look over your list and answer these questions:

- Are you beginning to recognize that you are partly responsible for your anger? Can you identify times when you were dishonest, selfish, self-seeking, fearful, or inconsiderate?
- Can you see that it's the actions—not people—that are "bad"?
- Do you see that as long as you hang on to anger, it will control you? Can you let go of resentments and clear space for love, patience, and tolerance toward yourself and others?

Describe how you feel about letting go of resentments. Can you imagine your life free from regret, pain, and anger about past events?

....

....

....

....

....

....

....

"Though no one can go back and make a brand new start,
anyone can start from now and make a brand new end."
—Carl Bard

Laugh a Little

A good laugh is good for you. It relieves tension and stress and helps you maintain a healthy mental outlook. Staying sober is hard work that challenges you mentally, physically, and spiritually, so remember to laugh, play, and celebrate your successes. When you laugh, you feel good, and feeling good helps you remember to be grateful for your sobriety and your recovery community.

Describe some things you could do to help you laugh this week. You might enjoy watching a funny movie or getting together with a fun friend.

....

....

....

....

....

....

....

....

....

....

....

"He who laughs, lasts."

Practice Recovery Slogans

These slogans are often practiced in Twelve Step groups:

- "One day at a time" reminds you that recovery is a journey taken one step at a time.
- "First things first" means your first commitment must be sobriety.
- "Easy does it" reminds you to avoid taking on too much, especially during early recovery.
- "Live and let live" means mind your own business. Focus on living your life and try not to control someone else or judge his or her progress.
- "Let go and let God" means when you've done all you can do, ask your Higher Power to help do the rest.
- "Accept life on life's terms" means to embrace life as it is, with all its imperfections.
- "Progress, not perfection" reminds you that recovery is a journey, not a destination, and that every step forward is success.
- "This, too, shall pass" is another way of saying only change is permanent.
- "Turn it over" means letting your Higher Power guide you.
- "Go with the flow" is practicing acceptance.
- "Keep it simple" reminds you not to get distracted by unimportant things.

Identify one of the recovery slogans that you can really relate to right now. Describe how this recovery slogan can help you stay on track. Take a minute to write the slogan down on a piece of paper, and place it in your car, on your refrigerator, on your bathroom mirror, or anywhere you will see it often.

....

....

....

....

....

"Slogans are wisdom written in shorthand."

Manage Anger

Anger is appropriate when people hurt you or when you witness injustice. However, sometimes you might hide behind anger to avoid uncomfortable feelings. For example, you might get angry about not having control over a situation, or you might use anger to isolate yourself when faced with grief, hurt, loss, or fear. When not managed, unresolved anger can threaten your sobriety. Apply the ABCD strategy to deal with anger:

A: Describe the ACTION or event that made you angry.
B: What BELIEFS or thoughts did you have?
C: Describe how you felt and what you did (CONSEQUENCES).
D: DISPUTE your thinking by asking, "Who said so? What is the evidence? Is there a more helpful way to look at things?"

Think about a time you were really angry. Use the ABCD method to describe the situation and identify a positive way to handle things. If you can't address the source of your anger directly and calmly, talk to your sponsor or a friend. Get your anger out by walking or writing in your journal. You can write a letter to the person you are angry with, but don't send the letter. Instead, destroy the letter and much of your anger will disappear with it. Do what you can to let anger go so it doesn't turn inward on you or explode outward later.

....

....

....

....

....

....

"Turn your wounds into wisdom."

Use HALT to Identify Your Feelings

It is difficult to identify your feelings in early recovery, but there are ways to make identification easier. A useful recovery tool is HALT: a cue to ask yourself whether you are hungry, angry, lonely, or tired. Any one of these feelings can lead you to incorrect, inappropriate, or just plain stinking thinking. If you experience more than one of the HALT feelings at the same time, you could be headed for real trouble. Pay attention to these four feelings, and if you feel them, make sure you eat, rest, and call your sponsor or a recovery friend.

Read what page 419 in *Alcoholics Anonymous* says about feelings. Take stock of how you feel today by using the HALT recovery tool. Are you hungry, angry, lonely, or tired? How can you change your diet, schedule, or attitudes to minimize these feelings?

"If a thought or belief doesn't serve you, let it go."

Let Go of Blame

Blame is a coping skill that addicts often use to avoid personal responsibility. Even if you are not to blame for something, you are responsible for your feelings about what happened. Think about it—when you blame others, you create an instant sense of inferiority, not just between you and the other person, but also between you and the world. It never truly feels good to blame other people. Blaming others allows you to hold on to anger and fear about how *you* feel about a situation.

Refuse to turn your anger and fear outward. Don't blame others for your own frustrations or unmet expectations. Old habits can be very hard to break. Try to take responsibility for your "side of the street" and let others do the same. When you let go of blame, you let go of past hurts and resentments, and take responsibility for your own expectations.

Before you can truly grow spiritually, you need to remove blame from your thoughts, actions, attitudes, and communications. Read page 297 in *Alcoholics Anonymous*. Describe a time when you blamed someone. How can you take responsibility for your feelings about the situation? Ask your sponsor, recovery group, and family to respectfully let you know when you fall back into blaming.

....

....

....

....

....

....

....

"Sweep your own side of the street."

Keep Working

By now you've spent a few months in recovery. Are you feeling more confident? Is your self-esteem growing? Do you feel like you could accomplish the things you set your mind to? If the answer is "yes" or even "sometimes," then you should give yourself some recognition for working hard enough to grow stronger in recovery. It's natural to have strong feelings of optimism about your new life. It's also natural that your feelings of confidence and dedication will change daily. Some days you may feel on top of the world, while other days may really challenge you.

If you find that your confidence has caused you to be less diligent in going to meetings, talking with your sponsor, meditating, and connecting with your Higher Power, then take this moment to give yourself a benevolent reality check: Remember that you have a body that can't handle alcohol or other drugs. You have a mind that can't give them up. You have a current spiritual condition that can't do anything about it. Working the Steps is a lifelong process that helps you address the body, mind, and spirit problem of addiction.

Describe a few things you can do this week to work harder on recovery.

....

....

....

....

....

....

....

....

"An idea that is developed and put into action is more important
than an idea that exists only as an idea."
—Buddha

Perform a Fears Inventory

The second part of Step Four is performing a fears inventory. Holding on to fear can keep you from knowing yourself, your Higher Power, or others as richly as is possible. A fears inventory can help you see how actions and attitudes play into your fears. As you change those things, you lessen your fear, which leaves more room for peace and serenity. Once you identify your fears, you can manage them if you take each slowly and accept that fear is normal. Remember to live each day at a time, rely on your Higher Power, and use the Twelve Steps and your recovery group for support.

List all the things that you fear. Next to each fear, write the cause of it. Be brief and don't overanalyze. Did the fear affect your self-esteem, pride, relationships, finances, emotional security, goals, or dreams? How can you begin to hand these fears over to your Higher Power? If these fears were not holding you back, what would your life look like?

....

....

....

....

....

....

....

....

....

"Strive for a little less fear and a lot more faith."

Trust the Journey

Consider this meditation: "The truly confident person knows that life is much more of a process and a journey than a matter of answers and destinations. We can accept the unknown in life or be paralyzed by what we don't know. If the open road makes us too frightened and insecure, we will probably miss all the lovely scenery along the way. And we won't learn the lessons of the journey. Confidence arises from self, not circumstances. Just because the road is uncertain doesn't mean that we are. If we have a Higher Power walking just ahead of us, we have all the security we need."

Have you ever taken a vacation and found that much of what made the experience rich were the surprises and unplanned experiences? Using your own words, describe what the above meditation means to you.

....

....

....

....

....

....

....

....

....

....

"Take time to smell the roses."

Have Sober Fun

When you were using, you probably didn't think anything could be fun if drinking and drugs weren't involved. You have a right to have a good time as a healthy, sober person. The more fun you have when you're sober, the less appealing it will be to go back to those days when you equated fun with being high.

Describe what sober fun means to you. How can you take time this week to have sober fun?

....

....

....

....

....

....

....

....

....

....

....

"If you're not having fun, you're doing something wrong."
—Groucho Marx

Review Your Fears Inventory

The Little Red Book has long served as a wise guide for newcomers to the Twelve Step program. *The Little Red Book* explains how addicts have a tendency to discount fear because they mistakenly associate it with cowardice. Yet, full knowledge of fear is essential to recovery. This is why performing an honest and complete fears inventory is an important part of not only your recovery but also your spiritual development.

As you review your list of fears, identify ways you contributed to or caused the fear. Describe some changes you can make to reduce your fears.

....

....

....

....

....

....

....

....

....

....

"Fear is nothing more or less than a distorted faith
in the negative things of life and the evils that might beset us."
—*The Little Red Book*

Stay Grounded

As you are discovering, recovery is about so much more than staying clean and sober. Your journey began with abstinence and then moved into the lifelong process that involves spiritual transformation. Each day you are becoming more the person you are meant to be. You are learning new ways of thinking, acting, feeling, and being. No matter how your life circumstances shift and change, you will stay grounded by knowing that your Higher Power is actively working in your life.

Quiet your mind and environment, breathe deeply, and take a moment to imagine yourself in recovery five years from now. You might picture yourself a little older but more deeply settled into recovery—happier and more serene. How does your recovery look and feel?

....

....

....

....

....

....

....

....

....

....

"I pray that I'll always seek guidance as my spiritual journey continues today."

Let Go of Worry

Very little of what we fear actually happens, which means that most of our fears cause us to worry unnecessarily. Doesn't it make sense to learn how to better cope with fear? The following strategies can help, but of course, if you fear for your safety, get help right away.

- Accept that fear is a normal and temporary way of feeling.
- Face your fears each day without using alcohol or other drugs.
- Remind yourself that worrying about things you can't control is a waste of time.
- Hand your fears over to your Higher Power.
- Use the Serenity Prayer (see Day 17) to let go of stress and worry.
- Keep working the Steps, especially when your motivation is low.
- Believe in yourself and in your recovery.
- Spend time in fun sober activities to take your mind off problems.

Describe your worst fear. How you can use these strategies to begin to relax and let go of this fear that's inhibiting your life?

....

....

....

....

....

....

....

....

"Living in fear is like paying interest on a loan you don't owe."
—Sandi Bachom

Connect with Others

Addiction can cause you to lose touch with yourself and others, so pay attention to the ways you interact with other people. Are you able to greet other people with a smile? Are you at ease at gatherings where you may not know anyone? Do you go out of your way to make others feel comfortable and welcome?

Some people in early recovery say that they have such strong feelings of pain, sadness, and anger that it is hard to smile and be open to others. If you feel this way, it's okay. Accept these feelings as your authentic experience today. But also be open to the idea that most emotions are temporary. Everyone has days of joy and days of sadness. As you spend more time in recovery, you will feel better and trust yourself more. If you change your thinking, your feelings will follow.

Go to a meeting this week and try to be open with another person. You may be focused on your own struggle, but let go of it for a few minutes. Ask another person about his or her day. Everyone is human and struggles with fear, anxiety, and sadness. But everyone is also capable of compassion, love, and peace. Start to be open to the beauty found even in everyday struggle. Embrace this humanity in yourself and in others.

What positive connections did you make today?

....

....

....

....

....

....

....

"Change your thinking and change your world."

Keep Overcoming Fear

Performing a fears inventory as a part of your Step Four work helps you see how facing your fears can make more room for courage. Your fears may be emotional, physical, or financial. Some of your fears may not make sense on a rational level. Nevertheless, they are real and powerful, and you should congratulate yourself for being brave enough to take a hard look at them.

Take your fears inventory a step deeper. Look at your list of fears. What part of you is most threatened by these fears? Is it your ego, self-esteem, pride, or security that is affected? Do you recognize patterns in the types of fears you have? What do you need to work on the most?

....

....

....

....

....

....

....

....

....

"The AA program . . . is a spiritual way of life based on . . .
a Power greater than ourselves *to overcome fear*
and other defects of our alcoholic personalities."
—*The Little Red Book*

Create Joy Every Day

How are you creating joy in your daily life? Are you counting your blessings and thanking your Higher Power for them? Are you taking the time to plan positive and uplifting things for yourself?

Like fun, joy has to be cultivated. You won't find it if you aren't seeking it. Look for joy in all the things you do daily—in your work, in your friends, in your family, in recovery meetings, in school, or in your backyard. Are others noticing your quest for joy? Is your joy contagious?

Write down every time you've felt joy in the last week. Are there situations in which you regularly found joy? Are there situations in which you didn't?

....

....

....

....

....

....

....

....

....

"We must be the change we wish to see in the world."
—Mohandas Gandhi

Begin a Sexual Harms Inventory

As uncomfortable as it may be, Step Four's "fearless and moral inventory" requires that you look honestly at the sexual harms in your life: how you may have hurt others and how others may have hurt you. This task is easier when you accept that everyone has problems with sex at one time or another. Performing an honest sexual harms inventory frees you to learn from the past so you can have future intimate relationships without guilt, shame, fear, or remorse.

List anyone who was hurt or adversely affected by your sexual behavior. Write down the cause of each sexual harm. For instance, you may have chosen to get high instead of being intimate with your partner or as a way to deaden the memory of a sexual harm that was done to you. Then, make a list of ways you have been hurt or threatened sexually.

Talk to your sponsor about how you can let go of these harms from the past. Learn about how to forgive harms done to you and ask forgiveness for harms you have done.

....

....

....

....

....

....

....

....

....

"Many of us needed an overhauling in regard to sex . . . Sex is never to be used lightly or selfishly, nor is it to be despised or loathed."
—*Twenty-Four Hours a Day,* August 24

Learn from Letting Go of Sexual Harms

Like resentments and fears, sexual harms also take up time and energy because they control you and keep you from your Higher Power. By making your sexual harms inventory, you begin to see how your actions and attitudes played into hurting others as well as yourself.

You can't erase the past, but you can learn from it so you don't repeat the same mistakes. An honest sexual inventory helps you deal with any pain you may have caused as well as the pain that may have been inflicted on you. A heavy burden is lifted, and your path to recovery is made clearer.

As you review your sexual harms inventory, do you recognize patterns? What kinds of people do you harm most often and in what unhealthy ways have you responded to others' harms? What sexual behavior was the most hurtful? You may notice that the more frequently a cause appears in your inventory, the more it tempted or controlled you.

"When I did my inventory, I noticed I wasn't all bad after all.
I am worthy of love."

Deal with Abuse

Abuse is the use (or threat of use) of physical, sexual, or verbal behavior to overpower or humiliate. The behavior, not degree of injury, determines abuse. Look at the descriptions of abuse below. If you've experienced abuse, talk with your therapist, sponsor, or recovery group about how it is affecting you *now*.

- Physical abuse includes being pushed, shoved, or hit; physically restrained; targeted with a thrown object; locked out of the home; abandoned in a dangerous place; denied basic physical needs; choked or burned; or threatened with a weapon.
- Sexual abuse is not only rape; it is any nonconsensual sexual behavior that humiliates. When a person is demeaned by negative remarks about the body; called degrading sexual names or treated as a sex object; forced to beg for sexual attention or watch or participate in pornography; or forced to do sexual acts, he or she has been sexually abused.
- Emotional abuse is meant to threaten, intimidate, and degrade and can include name-calling; frightening someone by looks, actions, or gestures; controlling by monitoring every move; disregarding concerns; or treating someone like a servant.

Have you experienced any of these forms of abuse? If you feel comfortable remembering the event, describe what happened and how you feel about it. It's hard to find a way to bring up the subject, but find someone you trust—your therapist, sponsor, or recovery friend—and start to talk about your feelings. Talking about what happened can often free you from the burden of hiding or suppressing your feelings.

....

....

....

....

....

"FEAR = Face Everything And Recover"

Keep Thinking Positively

You can't control anyone else's actions, but you can control your own reactions. There is usually something positive—a lesson to be learned, an insight to be gained—even in the bleakest of moments.

Describe a few recent things that challenged or broke down your positive outlook. Try to identify the moments when you felt your attitude shifting and emotions like anger, self-pity, fear, or anxiety taking hold. What parts of the situation were outside your control? What things could you have changed?

....

....

....

....

....

....

....

....

....

....

"Now I am more positive. I believe in people and in their capabilities.
There is much love and truth and honesty in the world . . .
Life now seems worthwhile and it is good to live."
—*Twenty-Four Hours a Day,* November 9

Keep Taking Responsibility for Harms

Although it's always easier to scrutinize others, Step Four is about honestly examining your own actions and reactions to see how your addiction has harmed others. Review your inventory work, specifically whom you have harmed and what harms you inflicted. What motivated you to cause the harm? Ask yourself which of the following parts of you directed your actions:

- self-image (how you think of yourself)
- pride (how you think others view you)
- emotional security (your general sense of well-being)
- finances (your basic desire for money, property, and possessions)
- ambitions (your goals, plans, and designs for the future)
- personal relationships
- sexual relations (your basic drive for sexual intimacy and gratification)

Record the feelings that motivated your hurtful acts. Were you dishonest, selfish, fearful, or inconsiderate? Then write down what you should have done instead for each situation.

....

....

....

....

....

....

"Nothing can bring you peace but yourself."
—Ralph Waldo Emerson

Let Go of Character Flaws

When you honestly examine all the harm your character flaws have caused, you start learning tolerance, patience, and goodwill toward others. The goal of recovery is to replace your anger, fear, and harms with their opposites. When you're able to cope with your anger, you become more understanding of others. When you let go of fear, you become more accepting of life. As you own up to the harm you have done to others, you become more capable of better choices in the future.

Take a moment to meditate on any shifts in attitude and behavior you are experiencing in your recovery journey. Describe any transformations—no matter how subtle—you have encountered so far. Thank your Higher Power for the miracle of recovery that is taking place within you.

"Live to learn; learn to live."

Congratulations for working on Step Four! You are beginning to be fearless. If you notice your old ways and thoughts resurfacing, go back and review the lessons you learned in this Step.

Follow the Path to Freedom

DAY 126 TO DAY 155

Admit Past Wrongs

Step Five: "Admitted to God, to ourselves, and to another human being the exact nature of our wrongs."

Step Four asked you to be honest and list your past wrongs. In Step Five, you "come clean" by sharing your inventory. While you might be okay admitting your character defects and wrongdoings to yourself and to your Higher Power, you may balk at telling them to someone you know. Acknowledging your mistakes helps develop accountability and humility. Step Five rids you of denial and requires you to take responsibility for your choices and their consequences. Once you admit your wrongs to someone, you can look the world in the eye without shame. You can accept that mistakes are a part of being human.

Remember, the person you choose to hear your Fifth Step—your sponsor, your friend, a member of the clergy—is there only to listen, not to give you absolution. Choose someone you trust.

....

....

....

....

....

....

....

....

....

"The elevator is broken; please use the Steps."

Prepare to Work Step Five

Step Five is a turning point where you begin to rid yourself of the obstacles that block you from your Higher Power. If you don't take responsibility for poor choices and admit mistakes, you might never overcome the compulsion to drink or use drugs.

Think about how you feel about your moral inventory. Is something holding you back from sharing your inventory with another person? If so, describe how you feel when you think about talking to another person about your wrongs. Talk to your sponsor to resolve any issues that are holding you back.

. . . .

. . . .

. . . .

. . . .

. . . .

. . . .

. . . .

. . . .

. . . .

. . . .

"The humility [Step Five] brings us is necessary to our future welfare.
We will have no spiritual inspiration, no release from anxiety and fear,
until we remove the skeletons from our closet."
—*The Little Red Book*

Face Your Fears

As this recovering person discovered, there is a big difference between writing something down and reading it out loud: "In my Fifth Step, I was resistant to talk about some of the people I had wronged. I kept asking, 'Why can't I just keep it between me and my Higher Power?' I finally learned to tell my story, saying, 'I caused these things.' Letting go of pride, I went for it, holding nothing back. Verbalizing my 'confession' to another person helped me develop a sense of accountability and humility. It told the world that I admit my flaws and acknowledge my mistakes. At the same time, I realized that mistakes are a part of being a normal human being who is still growing and learning more all the time."

Meditate on this person's story and describe how you feel about admitting your wrongs to another person. Why do you think this is a necessary element of Step Five?

....

....

....

....

....

....

....

....

....

"If [Step Five] seems difficult to you . . . remember you are no exception . . .
This reaction is nothing more than the reflexes of a dying alcoholic personality
trying to avoid reality."
—*The Little Red Book*

Refuse to Bargain

In the past, you've probably tried to bargain about your substance use by telling yourself things like "If I cut back or just switch drugs, I'll be fine" or "I'll only party on weekends." You may have thought you could make your life better by setting new rules for yourself. And this may have worked for a short time, but eventually, it erodes your recovery.

Take a few minutes and describe the ways you tried to set rules for your drug use. Can you see that bargaining is just another way you try to be in control and get what you want?

....

....

....

....

....

....

....

....

....

....

....

....

"If you have to control your drinking or drug use, chances are it's out of control."

Find Someone You Can Trust

Spend some time today thinking of people who could hear your moral inventory. You might want to consider someone who understands the Steps and how important they are to recovery. Look for someone you trust, who is a good listener. Ask people in meetings for recommendations. You might want to choose your sponsor, your mentor, or a member of the clergy.

List the names of at least five people you can trust. Cross off any people who do not understand addiction, recovery, and the Twelve Steps. Out of the people left on your list, who would be willing and available to listen to your inventory? Identify one person to work Step Five with and make an appointment to meet during the next two weeks. Don't put this task off—it's essential to your spiritual growth. Who will you choose to hear your moral inventory?

"Face your fears and prosper beyond bounds."

Let Go of Addictive Thoughts

Recovery offers a wonderful opportunity to grow up all over again and develop your true self. One way to become more you is to dispute addictive thoughts such as the following:

- My life should be pain-free.
- Everything should go my way.
- I should always be in control.
- Life should always be fair.
- I shouldn't need to ask for help.
- I shouldn't share my feelings with others.
- My needs aren't important.

Which of the following strategies could you use this week to overcome addictive beliefs?

- seek guidance from your Higher Power
- practice positive affirmations
- talk with your sponsor
- read the Big Book
- go to meetings
- pray and meditate
- connect with supportive people
- practice new ways of being

Describe your addictive thoughts. What strategies can you use this week to overcome them?

....

....

....

....

"HOW = Honesty, Openness, and Willingness"

Keep Building Trust

Building trust in relationships takes work and willingness. Do you pay attention to others? Are you truthful? Are you loving, selfless, and generous? Do you give back to others? Are you humble in your words and actions? Do you ask for advice and guidance? Do you forgive yourself and others?

Are there things you do that cause harm in your relationships? Are you obsessed with getting your own way and being right? Do you try to impress others? Do you pretend you're someone you're not?

Write down a list of relationships you care about, and describe how you're building (or rebuilding) trust in each. Also list character defects (if any) that are getting in the way of your attempts to build trust.

....

....

....

....

....

....

....

....

....

....

"Trust God, clean house, and help others."

Give Back to Your Body

Your body has been there for you through thick and thin, and it's the only one you've got. One way you can "give back" to your body is to eat right and exercise. When you eat right, your body becomes stronger and your brain chemistry can rebalance. Exercise releases endorphins—natural chemicals in your body that improve your mood and relax you—that make a relapse or return to use less likely. When you eat balanced meals, drink lots of water, and get enough rest, you'll be stronger and happier and feel more able to handle life's challenges.

Write down what you ate today, and list the exercise you performed this week. Plan time in your schedule for exercise—even if it's just a walk around the block—and think of some healthy meals you'll enjoy making.

"If anything is sacred, the human body is sacred."
—Walt Whitman

Be Open, Honest, and Accountable

Step Five helps you to let go of the fear, shame, and insecurities that plague most addicts. It will free you from things in the past that have kept you from moving on with your life in healthy ways. By taking responsibility for your mistakes, you can begin to accept yourself as you are now: a magnificent work in progress.

Once you have decided on the person who will hear your moral inventory, don't waste time. Explain to that person that you need to be open, honest, and accountable. Explain that this is one of the most critical steps in your recovery, and that his or her role is just to listen. Make sure you bring your written inventory and allow enough time to say what you need to say. Let go of your pride and hold back nothing.

After you perform Step Five, answer the questions on page 75 in *Alcoholics Anonymous* to see whether you are ready for Steps Six and Seven.

"Confession is good for the soul."
—Scottish Proverb

Pocket Your Pride

Step Five is your chance to "let it all out," to share your past so you no longer carry the heavy weight of secrets that threaten your sanity and sobriety. Remember that you don't do Step Five to please the listener; you do Step Five to heal yourself. So swallow your pride, be open and honest, and practice humility as you allow someone you trust to take a deeper look inside you. Step Five is more than a confession; it is a verbal declaration that you are ready to change and be changed.

Read pages 72–74 in *Alcoholics Anonymous* to learn why it's important to share your moral inventory with someone. The person to whom you tell your Step Four inventory should care about you, know about addiction, and be a good listener. This person is not there to counsel, judge, or take away the pain of your self-examination.

If you've already done Step Five, ask yourself whether your pride got in the way and prevented you from being completely honest. What, if anything, did you hold back? You can always go back and talk to the person again.

"No one ever choked to death by swallowing their pride."

Experience the Freedom of Step Five

Experience shows that those who don't do a Fifth Step are most likely to use again. Admitting your wrongs to another person can be very healing. You learn how to be real with others instead of hiding behind a mask of addiction. Doing Step Five also teaches humility as you reveal your authentic self to someone who cares about you and your recovery.

Page 75 in *Alcoholics Anonymous* teaches that when you do a complete Fifth Step, you will experience the following:

- You will be delighted.
- You can look the world in the eye.
- You can be alone at perfect peace and ease.
- Your fears will fall from you.
- You will begin to feel the nearness of your Higher Power.
- You will move from having certain spiritual beliefs to having spiritual experiences.

Describe the benefits and freedoms you've experienced from doing Step Five. If you haven't done Step Five, describe what's holding you back.

....

....

....

....

....

....

....

*"The metamorphosis from the alcoholic to the new AA personality
becomes more evident upon completion of Step Five."*
—*The Little Red Book*

Accept Others

After you learn to look within instead of fixing others, you're ready to practice acceptance. The Big Book teaches you that you cannot find serenity until you accept things and people as they are. Serenity comes when you concentrate on what attitudes you need to change instead of how the world needs to change. Learning acceptance doesn't mean you should try to change others to suit your taste. It means you should accept people as they are. When you focus on another person's negative qualities, those qualities grow larger, so why not focus instead on the good qualities? Your serenity will grow as you develop reasonable, appropriate expectations of others. Remember that everyone is a work in progress. No one is perfect.

Reflect for a moment on a current relationship that is growing in positive ways. Why do you think it is working? How does this relationship differ from a difficult one? Are you more honest and considerate in the positive relationship? How can you improve the difficult relationship?

....

....

....

....

....

....

....

....

....

"Our acceptance of others grows in proportion to our acceptance of ourselves."

Create Strategies to Cope with Loss

The actor Douglas Fairbanks Jr. once said, "I tried to drown my sorrows, but they floated." People grow old and die. Children leave home. Change happens. No one escapes loss, so it makes sense to have some strategies in place so you don't turn to drugs in an attempt to numb or escape feelings of grief. You grieve because you love. When you attempt to dull your grief in unhealthy ways, you also diminish your ability to feel love and joy.

Reflect on the ways you reacted to loss in the past. Describe the feelings that arise during challenging life events. Be proactive and talk with your sponsor about healthy ways you can deal with challenging emotions when they appear. Write down the names of a few people you can talk to when loss occurs.

....

....

....

....

....

....

....

....

"Grief is a messy, imperfect, and non-linear process with no rules
or time limits. Honoring our grief is a way to honor ourselves.
We don't have to do it perfectly, and we don't have to do it alone."

Continue to Build Self-Esteem

Recovery is about learning to accept and celebrate who you are. As your self-esteem grows, your confidence and self-worth grow stronger and your relationships grow healthier. Self-worth can't be earned. You always have worth and value in spite of your struggles—it comes with being human.

One way to build self-esteem is to get rid of negative self-talk. Make a list of the negative ideas you have about yourself such as "Nobody likes me" or "I never do anything right." Develop a list of positive statements that refute the negatives, like "I am a person many people like" or "I have done many things right."

Read the positive affirmations out loud every day. Look at them in the morning and before bed. Share them with a friend. Post them where you will see them daily. You *are* a person of worth.

....

....

....

....

....

....

....

....

....

"Unless I accept my virtues, I most certainly will be overwhelmed by my faults."
—Robert G. Coleman

Uncover Hidden Resentments

Consider this story from a cocaine addict who has fourteen months in recovery: "I'd been holding on to some of my resentments for years. I was mad that I made compromises for my husband. I felt cheated because I didn't get the promotion I wanted. I even resented myself because my addiction caused me to lose contact with someone important to me. In the old days, I would get drunk just to get back at someone. But that approach never worked. It was like punching myself in the stomach to get back at someone else. Now I realize that I can't always control what others do—but I can control how I respond. These days, I let my Higher Power guide my choices. I let go of resentment as soon as it starts to build. By forgiving others, I've learned to also forgive myself."

Reflect on this story. Is there an issue from the past that you have not forgiven? Describe what happened. List the feelings you have about the event. Does it make you angry, sad, outraged, or jealous? Talk with someone in your recovery group who can help you find the wisdom and grace to let this resentment go.

....

....

....

....

....

....

....

....

"Remember not only to say the right thing in the right place, but far more difficult still, to leave unsaid the wrong thing at the tempting moment."
—Benjamin Franklin

Repel Loneliness with Spirituality

Prayer and meditation are active interaction with your Higher Power. When you pray, you're talking to your Higher Power and asking for the strength you need to stay sober and grow as a person. When you meditate, you're listening and trying to learn what your Higher Power's will is for you.

When you pray, ask your Higher Power for the strength to cope with loneliness. Ask for help being alone without feeling lonely. Ask your Higher Power to help you improve your relationships so that you have the emotional support and friendship you need.

List the times, days, or situations where you find yourself feeling lonely. Make a commitment to do healthy things to fill that time, either by calling a friend or practicing prayer or meditation.

....

....

....

....

....

....

....

....

....

"When we're alone, with nobody to pat us on the back, we must turn to our Higher Power for help. Can I say 'Thy will be done'—and mean it?"
—Adapted from *Twenty-Four Hours a Day,* June 15

Stay Focused

Even though it's likely that you are starting to feel pretty good about your recovery progress, make sure you still take time to work the routines that keep you clean and sober and spiritually fit. For example, you might be tempted to work long hours to make up for time you missed while you were addicted. You might want to relax and watch TV or hang out with friends instead of going to your weekly Twelve Step meeting. Don't allow yourself to get so busy that you stop making time for weekly recovery tasks such as going to meetings, talking with your sponsor, and connecting to your Higher Power through prayer and meditation.

Describe a few common ways you notice yourself losing focus. Are any of your weekly activities getting in the way of your recovery commitments? List a few things you need to do this week to continue to be successful in recovery.

"At first, giving up liquor is a big enough job for all of us,
even with God's help. But later on, we can practice self-discipline
in other ways to keep a firm grip on our minds so that we don't start any
wishful thinking. If we daydream too much, we'll be in danger of slipping."
—*Twenty-Four Hours a Day,* May 9

Stay Honest

Now that you have been working on your recovery and making improvements in your life, you may notice that some of your relationships are blossoming while others wither. Be patient with these relationships. It can take time to heal some of the damage done while you were using.

Start by taking a daily inventory of the quality of your relationships. Are you being honest with your sponsor? With your Twelve Step group? With your family, spouse, or significant other? Are you being loving, supportive, and respectful with others? Are you harboring resentments?

*"Sharing draws others to you. Take all who come as sent by
your Higher Power, and give them a royal welcome."*
—Adapted from *Twenty-Four Hours a Day,* February 24

Learn How Addiction Affects Relationships

You've probably heard the saying "Addiction is a family disease." Like any illness, addiction causes confusion and a host of varied reactions from those who care about you. Friends and family may resent you for the hurt your addiction caused them or for the fear they felt when they worried they might lose you. Some loved ones may feel responsible for your addiction, or they may feel guilty or powerless because they couldn't help you.

Your friends and family can heal during your recovery. Each person must concentrate on his or her own issues while learning how to detach with love. Al-Anon is a Twelve Step group that supports families and friends of alcoholics and other addicts. Parents, children, spouses, partners, siblings, other family members, friends, employers, employees, and co-workers of addicts can attend Al-Anon meetings. All these people have something in common: their lives have been affected by someone else's drinking or drug use.

Describe how your use of alcohol and other drugs has affected your friends and family. Spend a moment meditating on how you can help these relationships to thrive.

....

....

....

....

....

....

....

....

"Addiction affects the whole family, but so does recovery."

Give Thanks for the Courage to Work Step Five

After you have completed Step Five, page 75 in *Alcoholics Anonymous* advises you to return home and find a place where you can be quiet for an hour so you can contemplate the full significance of what you have accomplished. You have shared your wrongs with your Higher Power and another person, and you have honestly owned them yourself. Along the way, you discovered that facing your past and admitting your mistakes didn't kill you. Those who love you and support your recovery did not run away in disgust or pass judgment on you.

Completing Step Five is a cause for true thanksgiving. Do as the Big Book suggests and spend an hour in deep reflection. Describe how you are feeling now that you've done Step Five. To whom and for what are you grateful? Don't forget to put your own name on that list for a difficult job well done. If you haven't worked Step Five yet, describe your difficulty in moving forward with this Step. Talk to your sponsor this week about what's holding you back.

"Let us rise up and be thankful, for if we didn't learn a lot today, at least we learned a little, and if we didn't learn a little, at least we didn't get sick, and if we got sick, at least we didn't die; so let us all be thankful."
—Buddha

Advocate for Your Health

You may not be aware that some over-the-counter (OTC) or prescription medication can compromise your sobriety. You may wonder which medications are safe for recovering people. Can you take a sleeping pill if you have insomnia? What about OTC medications for allergies?

Some recovering people must take medications to treat chronic pain, allergies, or other medical conditions. While many medications are safe, others should not be used by people in recovery because they can trigger the memory of being high, which can cause cravings and relapse.

Write down the names of all OTC and prescription medications that you use. Make a commitment to talk with your doctor, pharmacist, and sponsor to identify nonaddictive medicines that you can use to treat your symptoms.

....

....

....

....

....

....

....

....

....

"Every man is the builder of a Temple called his body."
—Henry David Thoreau

Keep Laughing

Perhaps you've heard the story of the man who laughed himself back to health when he got a cancer diagnosis. You can't laugh yourself to successful recovery, but laughter will help you find peace in the midst of chaos. Take some time this week to participate in light, fun activities. Go see a stand-up comedian, catch a funny movie, or read a funny book.

Think about the friends who have always made you laugh. If they are sober friends who support your recovery, they can give you a lift and help you to enjoy your newfound clarity and sobriety.

Write down some fun activities you can do or names of friends who always make you laugh. Schedule something that will make you laugh at least once a week.

"I pray that I may strive for inward peace. I pray that I may not be seriously upset, no matter what happens around me."
—*Twenty-Four Hours a Day,* July 28

Try New Things

In your using days, you may have felt anxious or fearful about trying new things. You may have felt especially anxious about facing a challenging social situation, such as starting a new job or going to a class or event where you don't know anyone.

As you work the Steps, you will grow more confident in your abilities. This is appropriate because now that you are sober, you can do many things that seemed impossible when you were using alcohol or other drugs.

When you feel ready, adopt an attitude of adventure. Open yourself up to healthy and safe new things and experiences. There is an exciting new world for you to discover. Set out to experience it sober. The added bonus is that you'll remember it afterward!

Take a moment and think about things you would like to do that you may not have attempted before. Have you always wanted to ride a horse? Have you been tempted to take an astronomy class or join a book group? Is there a friend who has a hobby you might like to pursue? New experiences don't need to be risky or expensive—just things that feed the steady growth that's already begun.

....

....

....

....

....

....

....

"I'm not afraid of storms, for I'm learning how to sail my ship."
—Louisa May Alcott

Keep Working on Character Defects

Almost all character defects come from

- a lack of acceptance
- a lack of willingness
- a lack of humility
- a need to control
- a deep fear
- a sense of shame

Describe the defects of character that you think keep you from being the person you want to be and prevent you from connecting deeply with your Higher Power. Review your list and focus on two or three that you want to work on at this point in your recovery. Share your list with your sponsor or a recovery friend. Work together to find patterns so you will better know how to make progress.

....

....

....

....

....

....

....

"The strongest principle of growth lies in the human choice."
—George Eliot

Strengthen Your Spirituality

The truth is, you are always only one drink or hit away from relapse. The good news is that the spiritual focus you are finding will help you maintain your sobriety one day at a time. Read pages 85–88 in *Alcoholics Anonymous* to learn about the value of maintaining a spiritual focus. Ask yourself the following questions each night before you go to bed:

- Was I resentful, selfish, dishonest, or afraid?
- Do I owe an apology to anyone?
- Have I kept something to myself that should be discussed with another person at once?
- Was I kind and loving toward all?
- What could I have done better?
- Was I drifting into worry, remorse, or morbid reflection?

Write down your answers, then ask your Higher Power for guidance. Remember to celebrate your daily successes, and consider sharing your answers with your sponsor or a recovery friend.

....

....

....

....

....

....

....

"When self-examination, meditation, and prayer are interwoven,
the result is an unshakable foundation for life."
—*Twelve Steps and Twelve Traditions*

Embrace Honesty

Addicts live in a world of deceit and denial. Recovery calls on you to be honest with yourself, your family and friends, and all others you have harmed. This requires you to speak the truth, but always with compassion. Never use honesty to purposely hurt someone. If you struggle with balancing honesty and compassion, talk with your sponsor or recovery group and ask your Higher Power to grant you the wisdom you need to speak compassionate truth. Making small, daily choices to be kind and honest will help you grow spiritually.

Write down three recent situations in which you told the truth to someone. Was this compassionate truth-telling? What does compassionate honesty mean to you?

....

....

....

....

....

....

....

....

....

"[Honesty is] freedom from self-deception; trustworthiness in thought
and action; sincerity in our desire to recover from alcoholism;
willingness to admit a wrong; fairness in all our dealings with others;
refusal to sneak that first drink."
—*The Little Red Book*

Move Through Mistakes

When you make a mistake, don't look back at it for very long. Mistakes are lessons of wisdom. The past cannot be changed. The future is in your power.

If you have recently made a mistake or neglected your recovery, it's important to take immediate steps to remedy the situation. Make a new commitment this week to talk to your sponsor or recovery group about any mistakes you've made. They will offer wisdom and help you move forward.

Describe a recent mistake you made. What parts of the situation did you have control over? What could you have done differently to create a more positive outcome?

....

....

....

....

....

....

....

....

....

....

"I am only one; but still I am one. I cannot do everything,
but still I can do something. I will not refuse to do the something I can do."
—Helen Keller

Acknowledge Defects and Strengths

The Big Book describes character defects as "flaws in our make-up which caused our failure" that stem from self-centeredness. While addicts and nonaddicts have character defects, these flaws, especially if left unattended, can lead to relapse. Chief among an addict's character defects is resentment, which the Big Book calls "the 'number one' offender." Fear, lying, all forms of denial (including minimizing, rationalizing, and blaming), grandiosity, and self-pity are other common defects of chemically dependent people.

You listed your character defects in Step Four, and you admitted them in Step Five. Don't forget to do an honest assessment of your strengths too. Sometimes in the midst of intense self-examination, it's harder for you to name what's good about yourself. But this practice helps you chart your growth and accept yourself as the splendid human being you are.

Today, concentrate on your strengths by writing down only positive things about yourself. If you are willing, explain this exercise to a recovery friend and share your list.

....

....

....

....

....

....

....

....

"God doesn't make junk."

Understand Dreams about Using

Although your dreams may be intense and even frightening, it is very common to dream about using, especially in early recovery. Often, these dreams seem very real and can create powerful feelings that last into the following day. As you grow stronger in recovery, these dreams will happen less often.

Frequently, these dreams are about deciding whether or not to use. When you review these types of dreams, you often get valuable hints that can help you avoid relapse. The dreams may reveal situations that pose a danger to your sobriety.

Describe a recent dream. Does the dream help you understand yourself better?

....

....

....

....

....

....

....

....

....

....

....

....

"All dreams are in service of the dreamer."

Celebrate Your Progress

Completing the Fourth and Fifth Steps are huge milestones in your recovery. Great job! At this point, you have most likely made a lot of progress. You may have found yourself

- experiencing periods of serenity
- speaking more at meetings
- doing service for others
- applying the Steps to situations
- realizing that you don't need to use in order to cope with problems
- being more accountable to family, friends, work, and so on
- focusing on your role in problems and working on problem-solving
- realizing that you are not responsible for others—you can only change yourself

Review this list of changes and write down the ones you've experienced thus far in your recovery. What other progress have you noticed? Review the list with your sponsor or your recovery group. Ask whether they've observed other changes as well.

....

....

....

....

....

....

"The world is a great mirror. It reflects back to you what you are.
If you are loving, if you are friendly, if you are helpful, the world
will prove loving and friendly and helpful to you. The world is what you are."
—Thomas Dreier

Congratulations for working on Step Five! You are beginning to follow the path to freedom. If you notice your old ways and thoughts resurfacing, go back and review the lessons you learned in this Step.

Prepare to Change

DAY 156 TO DAY 185

Prepare for Steps Six and Seven

Step Six: "Were entirely ready to have God remove all these defects of character." Step Seven: "Humbly asked Him to remove our shortcomings."

In Steps Four and Five, you laid down a heavy burden by admitting past wrongs, and you took responsibility by sharing your moral inventory. With Steps Six and Seven, you ask your Higher Power to remove your shortcomings. When you do this, you are saying, "I don't want to be what I was. I am ready for change." You are admitting that you cannot make these changes on your own. This action deepens the surrender you experienced in Steps One through Three.

Close your eyes, breathe deeply, and meditate about the person you long to be. Describe what you see.

....

....

....

....

....

....

....

....

....

....

"Nothing changes if nothing changes."

Get Ready for Change

Step Six asks you to become "entirely ready" to have your Higher Power remove your character defects. This is an act of faith. You are the clay, and your Higher Power is the sculptor who will mold you into the extraordinary being you are meant to be. Your old and destructive patterns have been "hardwired" into your personality. It takes a "new you" to respond to the world in different ways. Before this can happen, you need to be entirely ready for positive change.

Meditate about the values you want to live by. Describe these in detail. Take stock of your current behaviors. Ask yourself every day, "Are my actions in line with my values?"

....

....

....

....

....

....

....

....

....

....

"We cannot divide our lives into compartments and keep some for ourselves.
We must give all the compartments to our Higher Power."
—Adapted from *Twenty-Four Hours a Day,* August 26

Act with Integrity

When you are ready to have your character defects removed, you acknowledge that you are willing to act differently. This willingness requires an attitude adjustment. In the past, you may have made a habit of blaming others or dwelling on your unmet needs. In Step Six, you become willing to have those attitudes and approaches altered permanently. Many times, it's the little ways in which you are selfish, thoughtless, or dishonest that are the hardest to give up because you "get away with it." This is the attitude you confront in Step Six. As long as you think you can get away with something, you hold on to a remnant of your addiction.

Review your inventory and imagine your Higher Power taking away all your short-comings. Which things are hardest for you to give up?

....

....

....

....

....

....

....

....

....

"We all come before God as sick people. We offer no alibis.
We have no defense. We ask for wisdom and understanding.
We ask forgiveness for the wrongs we have committed. Acknowledging
our shortcomings, we sincerely pray to God that he will remove them."
—Adapted from *The Little Red Book*

Change Old Behaviors

The spiritual transformation that Twelve Step living offers is life-altering and requires major behavioral changes. You may discover that you can't hang out with your old drinking or using buddies. You might recognize the temptations inherent in placing yourself in high-risk situations or in going to places where you know drugs will be present. In addition, you are probably discovering that personal traits like anger and self-centeredness can trigger your desire to use again.

Identify some behavioral changes you need to make in order to maintain your abstinence and strengthen your recovery. For each change, list two or more action steps you can take to make the change happen, such as cut ties with users or meditate to lessen resentment.

....

....

....

....

....

....

....

....

*"When I see these men and women get sober and stay sober . . . I know
that A.A. works. The change I see in people . . . convinces me that there
must be a Power greater than ourselves which helps us to make that change."*
—*Twenty-Four Hours a Day,* April 23

Trust in the Promises

Pages 83–84 in *Alcoholics Anonymous* promise that if you diligently work the Twelve Steps, you will

- be amazed at your recovery progress
- know a new freedom and happiness
- not regret the past
- understand true serenity and peace
- see how your experience can benefit others
- be rid of feelings of uselessness and self-pity
- put aside selfishness and reach out to help others
- let go of self-seeking attitudes and behavior
- improve your attitude about life
- be free from the constraints of fear
- intuitively know how to handle situations that used to baffle you
- realize that your Higher Power is doing for you what you could not do for yourself

Read these promises and describe the one that is most difficult for you to believe at this point in your recovery. What needs to happen for you to believe this promise? What is holding you back? Discuss your thoughts and feelings with your sponsor.

....

....

....

....

....

"We came, we came to, and then we came to believe."

Practice Spirituality

Spirituality isn't always about religion or a Higher Power. Spirituality can also come from meaningful connections with people or nature. Calling your sponsor can be spiritual. Reaching out to a supportive sober friend can be spiritual. Helping to find a home for an abandoned puppy can be spiritual. When your intentions are spiritual, your daily actions and interactions are spiritual.

Reach out with spiritual intention. Call your sponsor. Call a supportive friend or family member. Call someone from your recovery group. Reach out with a small act of kindness to a stranger.

Did you practice spirituality today? Describe what you did and how it felt. Think about how you can be more spiritual in your daily life, even if it's just taking time to bring a cup of coffee to a friend.

"I will practice spirituality by treating all people with dignity and respect."

Remember Why Recovery Is Important

Take time to remind yourself why you continue to choose a new path for your life. Do you want more peace and serenity? Do you want a better life for yourself and your family? Do you want to be a better parent, sibling, or friend? Do you want to better manage your responsibilities and finances?

Write a detailed list of things you are grateful for. What have you gained since you have been in recovery? What can you gain in the future? Put a copy of the list in your wallet, in your car, or on your bathroom mirror so you are reminded daily of the gifts of recovery.

"I can give my life greater meaning by how I choose to live every day."

Focus on Health

Once you're ready to add physical health to your daily routine, consider your diet. Is it low in fat with plenty of protein, complex carbohydrates, and fiber? Does it include nuts or legumes, fish, vegetables, fruit, poultry, eggs, and dairy products? It's also good to limit your consumption of refined carbohydrates, such as white bread or white rice, and foods containing saturated fat, such as red meat.

Take brisk walks, work in your garden, or ride your bike. Try yoga, karate, or other activities that improve your balance and strength. Go swimming or take a dance class. Whatever activity you do, performing thirty minutes of cardiovascular exercise a day is great for your health.

Keep a record of how you feel physically from day to day. Note which foods make you feel the best, and what impact exercise has on how you feel. Are there changes you can make in order to feel better?

....

....

....

....

....

....

....

....

"Health is the greatest gift, contentment the greatest wealth,
faithfulness the best relationship."
—Buddha

Accept Your Life Today

Recovery doesn't eliminate all of life's challenges, but it gives you the tools to deal with them. The Serenity Prayer says "God, grant me the serenity to accept the things I cannot change, the courage to change the things I can, and the wisdom to know the difference." These powerful words contain all that is necessary for acceptance: letting go, tolerance, powerlessness, surrender, and faith. Here are some ways recovering people have defined acceptance:

- "Acceptance is gratitude."
- "Acceptance is love."
- "Acceptance means forgiveness."
- "When I accept something, I receive it willingly."
- "Acceptance means being at peace with something that once deeply troubled me."
- "Acceptance is the answer to all of my problems."

Recite the Serenity Prayer, then describe your idea of acceptance. Each and every day, you can either accept the reality that you experience, or you can attempt to control that reality by trying to get your way. Are you accepting today's reality?

....

....

....

....

....

....

....

"We cannot direct the wind, but we can adjust the sails."

Cultivate Friendships That Strengthen Self-Esteem

One way to build self-esteem is through healthy relationships with people who support your recovery. It is important to have people in your life who love you just as you are. It helps if you practice being this type of support person for others.

List a few people who support and accept you just as you are. How can you be more supportive and accepting in these relationships? How can you focus more on the positive? How can you be less controlling?

_____

_____

_____

_____

_____

_____

_____

_____

_____

_____

_____

"I'm thankful for recovery because it gave me my identity back.
Before recovery, I was whoever you needed me to be.
Now I can be myself, and that is okay."

Keep Celebrating Your Progress

Have you ever attended a recovery event that included a "recovery countdown"? The facilitator asks everyone in the audience to stand up. Then he or she asks those with the longest time sober—sometimes it's as many as fifty years or more—to sit down. Next, those with forty years or more will sit, and so on, until those with less than one year of sobriety remain standing. The facilitator continues the countdown until a person with only a few days of sobriety is left standing.

With each group that remains standing, the applause is enthusiastic and heartfelt, especially for those who are new to recovery. The point is that *any* amount of time in recovery—whether one day or fifty years—marks progress worthy of celebration.

Write down how many months or days you have been sober. If you are really ambitious, calculate your sober time in minutes. Give yourself credit for this success, and know that each day sober is a day closer to the serenity you seek.

....

....

....

....

....

....

....

....

....

"It's far easier to stay *sober than it was to* get *sober."*

Meditate on Recovery

Sit quietly for a moment and reflect on what being in recovery means to you. Are you noticing new sights, smells, and feelings? Is the sky a little brighter? Does food taste a little better? Do you notice nice things that others do for you? Do you notice a stronger connection with children, family, or friends?

Do you think you would have noticed these things if you were using alcohol or other drugs? Describe the new sensations you have discovered since you've quit using.

....

....

....

....

....

....

....

....

....

....

....

"I will be renewed. I will be remade. In this, I need God's help."
—*Twenty-Four Hours a Day,* January 3

Face Lingering Resentments

Consider this story about an alcoholic: John's resentment toward his wife, Linda, is slowly building. He often wonders, "Does she really love me? How important am I to her? Does she care about me at all?" These doubts are slowing eating away at the marriage, while John feels more hurt, offended, and wronged every day. He swallows his feelings because he's too insecure to share them with Linda. He thinks that if she really loved him, she would intuitively know how he feels. Feeling more and more like the self-righteous victim, John feels justified when he goes on drinking binges to drown his pain. He believes that he has done all he can and that he should wait for Linda to reach out and make things right between them.

Healing our resentments is up to us. Each of us must "clean our own side of the street" and take responsibility for our part in our relationships. Often, others are unaware of our feelings, or they might not even think there is a problem.

Write down what you think John could do to let go of his growing resentment toward Linda. Meditate about any resentments you might be harboring. What can you do to let them go for good?

....

....

....

....

....

....

....

....

"Resentment is like drinking poison and then hoping it will kill your enemies."

Make Time to Play

It's important for you to know that you're still fun to be around, even when you are sober. But now, people get to know you for who you really are.

Make a date with a friend or significant other to do something special that you wouldn't ordinarily do. Go to a play or a book reading. Go play catch with a football or race go-carts.

List a few people you'd like to spend some quality time with. Call each person and make some plans. Describe how it feels to care for yourself in this proactive way.

....

....

....

....

....

....

....

....

....

....

"When you actually schedule time for yourself, you just might convince yourself you deserve it. Plus you are modeling something invaluable to your children: the importance of tenderness to self."

Take Responsibility

Performing a moral inventory in Step Four helped you take responsibility for who you've been, who you are, and who you are becoming. You can take responsibility in other ways, such as attending Twelve Step meetings, spending time with your sponsor, and connecting with your Higher Power. It's not your sponsor's responsibility to get you to meetings or to make you work the program. It's yours.

You may struggle with the fact that some people don't yet trust the "new" you, but your actions will soon convince them that you are serious about improving your life. Being responsible builds others' confidence in you, and soon they will believe you are serious about your commitments to them and to the Twelve Step program.

Read about responsibility on pages 58 and 64 in *Alcoholics Anonymous*. Write five statements about responsibility beginning with the phrase "I am responsible for . . ."

....

....

....

....

....

....

....

....

....

"Although we are not responsible for our disease, we are responsible for our recovery."

Practice Self-Examination

Self-examination can be uncomfortable at first because you are used to your old ways of thinking and behaving. You may worry that if you give up some of your character defects, you won't be left with any personality at all. You may have protected yourself by being "quirky" or have grown fond of being accepted as "edgy" or "macho."

Remember that when your Higher Power removes your character defects, new character strengths will take their place. Selfishness, anxiety, and anger will be replaced with love, compassion, and serenity.

List the character defects you are having difficulty letting go of. Talk with your sponsor about why you are hanging on to these defects.

....

....

....

....

....

....

....

....

....

"Character defects stand between us and contented sobriety. They perpetuate spiritual illness. Recovery from alcoholism is dependent upon their removal."
—*The Little Red Book*

Let Go of Character Defects

Step Six: "Were entirely ready to have God remove all these defects of character."

Step Six asks you to become ready to have your Higher Power remove your character defects. This continues the "spiritual housecleaning" you began in Steps Four and Five. When you work Step Six, you become even more honest, humble, and willing to seek your Higher Power's help. Are you struggling with any of these character defects?

- lack of acceptance
- lack of willingness
- pride
- control
- fear
- shame
- intolerance
- self-centeredness
- resentment
- greed
- jealousy
- dishonesty
- self-pity
- other:

It's common to struggle with the idea of giving up all your character flaws. You may have used some of these defects to protect you from dealing with tough emotions. Other defects may just seem like too much fun to give up. Describe any defects you are hesitant to part with and share your thoughts with your sponsor or a friend in recovery.

....

....

....

"WILLING = When I Live Life, I Need God"

Break Old Habits

How do you undo habits that harm you and replace them with habits that help you? When times are tough, it is common to fall back into your old ways of thinking and acting.

Become willing to change. Evaluate the ways you usually act, react, think, and feel. Give yourself permission to grow and change. Ask for help from your Higher Power, your sponsor, and those who support you. Talk. Listen. Read. Practice new ways of being until they become second nature.

What things can you do to cultivate positive habits that benefit your sobriety and your spiritual growth? Are you willing to turn every day of your life over to your Higher Power? Could you practice daily affirmations? Read Twelve Step literature? What else could you do?

....

....

....

....

....

....

....

....

....

....

"We are what we repeatedly do. Excellence, then, is not an act, but a habit."
—Aristotle

Enjoy the Rewards of Acceptance

Consider the Serenity Prayer: "God, grant me the serenity to accept the things I cannot change, the courage to change the things I can, and the wisdom to know the difference." When you accept what you cannot change, you will find wisdom, courage, and peace. According to the Big Book, you will know a new freedom and happiness when you practice acceptance. You will not regret the past or wish to block it out through shame or guilt. Wisdom, freedom, happiness, no regrets, and serenity are certainly things worth striving for!

Read pages 207 and 416–417 in *Alcoholics Anonymous* to learn about accepting people, places, things, and situations as they are. Describe the rewards you have already experienced when you have practiced acceptance.

....

....

....

....

....

....

....

....

....

....

"The basis of all our prayers is: Thy will be done."
—*Twenty-Four Hours a Day,* August 29

Fill the Void

At first, using alcohol or other drugs may have felt like a positive thing. It may have masked anxiety or depression. It may have helped you feel like a more confident person, someone who fit in more. Or it may have removed all feelings, so you were numb to pain or trauma. Now that you've stopped using, you may feel a void. You may find that, like other addicts, you have been leading a double life. You may discover that you have created an "actor" that you present to the outer world. This actor is the person you want others to see, but in your heart, you know it isn't you.

Read pages 72–74 in *Alcoholics Anonymous* to learn why so many addicts create an actor. Describe your actor. How did creating the actor benefit you? Was it to avoid rejection or to cover up who you really are? Is your actor still there, lingering in the background? What can you do to be more honest and authentic?

....

....

....

....

....

....

....

....

"To thine own self be true."
—William Shakespeare

Keep Improving Relationships

Addiction damages relationships. You build relationships by

- being truthful
- asking your Higher Power for help
- respecting others
- practicing humility, gratitude, and forgiveness
- being loving, generous, and selfless

You break relationships by

- needing to be right or get your way
- needing to have your needs met first
- pretending to be someone you aren't
- being unwilling to share feelings
- sacrificing your needs to please others

    Think about your closest relationship, whether with a spouse, significant other, parent, sibling, or friend. What is going well? In what ways can you work to improve the relationship? How can you be more accepting and focus more on the positive? How can you be less controlling? Are your expectations reasonable?

....

....

....

....

....

"You can make more friends in two months by becoming interested in other people than you can in two years by trying to get other people interested in you."
—Dale Carnegie

Practice Willingness

Step Six is about adopting an attitude of willingness and trusting your Higher Power to help you figure out what needs to be changed and how to change it. Sometimes change occurs when you get out of your Higher Power's way and let divine things happen. You will find a new sense of peace when you are able to place your character defects in the hands of your Higher Power.

Describe some recent ways you have practiced willingness. Can you think of times you've stepped back, let go of control, and let things evolve as your Higher Power sees fit?

....

....

....

....

....

....

....

....

....

....

"Sometimes you find just what you need when you stop looking so hard."

Manage Anger

Anger isn't inherently destructive and shouldn't be feared. Anger is a normal, often useful, emotion that can motivate you to make necessary changes. You can manage anger in healthy ways when you

- remember to be responsible for your own feelings.
- don't let anger build to resentment.
- use honest language instead of name-calling, put-downs, or physical attacks.
- get to know yourself better by identifying the events and behaviors that trigger your anger.
- take care of your own needs. Know when you are hungry, angry, lonely, or tired (HALT), and put yourself on a regular schedule for meals, exercise, and rest.
- deal with frustrating issues as soon as possible.

What triggers your anger? What usually happens when you're angry? What could you do differently to create a more positive outcome?

....

....

....

....

....

....

*"Alcoholics are not saints . . . we will still feel and experience anger. The
important thing is to check yourself from venting anger unjustly upon someone
else, or from holding on to anger and letting it turn into a resentment, or
from turning it inward upon yourself so you feel unworthy and depressed."*
—*The Little Red Book*

Embrace Authentic Joy

When you were using, you may have become the expert at faking happiness. You may have used alcohol or drugs to "medicate" or numb feelings of grief or anger. The problem with numbing challenging feelings is that it also numbs your experience of happiness, joy, and peace.

Like laughter, joy helps your recovery by relieving stress and tension, allowing you to celebrate the good things in life. To rediscover joy, work the Steps and practice prayer and meditation. Pay attention to your relationships with others and work on building (or rebuilding) them. As you grow spiritually, you'll have more joy in your daily life.

Describe a time when you've felt pure happiness. How can you be more joyful in your daily life?

....

....

....

....

....

....

....

....

"In A.A., we get a real kick: not a false feeling of exhilaration,
but a real feeling of satisfaction with ourselves, self-respect,
and a feeling of friendliness toward the world."
—*Twenty-Four Hours a Day,* February 2

Keep Practicing Trust

Recovery can't happen without trust. You need the support, encouragement, wisdom, and strength of other addicts. Without that help, you're on your own again. So listen to those who have more experience in sobriety than you do. They can give you perspective and objectivity. Practice trusting your sponsor, your recovery group, and your Higher Power.

You may be worried about how people will react to you or what they think of you. You may be scared to trust, and that's okay. Just remember that where you've been (active addiction) is much more dangerous than where you are now (healthy recovery). Take healthy risks like starting a conversation with someone new or sharing your feelings. See what happens.

Read pages 542–543 in *Alcoholics Anonymous*. List some ways you can practice trust today.

....

....

....

....

....

....

....

....

....

....

"SWAT = Surrender, Willingness, Acceptance, Trust"

Affirm Yourself and Your Recovery

You can affirm yourself and your recovery by

- working the Twelve Steps
- reading meditation books and focusing on empowering thoughts
- attending recovery groups or events
- giving yourself new messages and cultivating new beliefs
- writing down affirmations of the positive life you envision
- surrounding yourself with people who support our recovery
- getting a massage, doing yoga, or taking another positive action because you deserve it
- celebrating your successes with others
- affirming others—finding out about their dreams and goals and supporting them
- placing affirmations in key places, such as on your desk or refrigerator, so you will think about them on a daily basis

Review this list and describe the ways you intend to affirm yourself and your recovery today.

....

....

....

....

....

....

"Three months out of drug treatment, I'd come home from work,
curl up on the sofa, and cry. Then I'd turn on the music and dance.
It felt exactly right. Crying, dancing, and then off to AA."

Set Recovery Goals

Goal-setting is a way to renew your commitment to recovery. You may want to make changes in your career or education, improve your financial life, improve relationships, get more involved in recovery, or reach out and serve others. Be sure to create smart goals that are specific, measurable, achievable, and realistic. Do this by

- identifying the goal (for example, "I will lead a Twelve Step meeting")
- setting a deadline
- listing obstacles you must overcome
- listing skills you need to accomplish your goal
- developing a plan and writing it down (you may want to share this with a recovery friend)
- listing the benefits of achieving the goal

Take a minute and identify a one-month, three-month, and one-year goal. Keep it simple, such as "In one month I will send thank-you notes to people in my support network." Include at least one goal where you reach out and serve others. Review your goals each month and repeat this process often.

"Don't judge each day by the harvest you reap but by the seeds that you plant."
—Robert Louis Stevenson

Be Patient

Addicts are often impatient people, but recovery is a lifetime journey, so take it slowly. Relax, breathe deeply, and try to appreciate that it may take years for you to digest all the profound changes you are experiencing. Drug use may have conditioned you to expect instant gratification in all things. But now you are discovering that each day is a blessing that slowly reveals itself if you just pay attention. Each minute is a new opportunity to practice living as a healthy, hopeful, spiritual being.

One way to practice patience is to keep letting go of expectations and judgments that trick you into thinking you know best. Remember that it is your Higher Power—not you—who should be at the steering wheel. And your Higher Power doesn't wear a watch.

Describe some recent ways in which you were patient. Are you holding on to any unreasonable expectations?

. . . .

. . . .

. . . .

. . . .

. . . .

. . . .

. . . .

. . . .

. . . .

"The greatest prayer is patience."
—Buddha

Work Toward Wisdom

Have you ever watched a child learn? Children come into the world as blank slates, not knowing how to speak or walk or grasp things. Soon they crawl, and then one day, they take a few steps on their own and off they go. Recovery is like that. You don't gain instant wisdom. You must work the Steps, seek guidance from your Higher Power, ask your sponsor and recovery group for help, and read the Big Book. Eventually, page by page, step by step, prayer by prayer, you will grow stronger and wiser.

Describe how working the Steps has improved your quality of life. What concepts or ideas have been most helpful to you? What wisdom have you gained?

....

....

....

....

....

....

....

....

....

....

"Wisdom is not a product of schooling but of the lifelong attempt to acquire it."
—Albert Einstein

Break Through Barriers

Right now you may have a hard time believing that you are capable of living a truly spiritual life. It helps to practice affirmations that will help overcome any negative thoughts that are holding you back.

Write a few affirmations to help you grow and change in positive ways. Following are some examples of helpful affirmations:

- I give myself permission to continue to grow and change.
- The past does not have a hold on me or define who I am now.
- I am more than my addiction.
- I can become the person I want to be.
- I allow others to take responsibility for their own lives.
- I do everything I need to keep myself healthy, fit, and peaceful.
- Each day I become more organized in all areas of my life.
- I accept that I can make mistakes and still keep trying.

Describe how affirmations can help you make good choices in daily life. Carry your affirmations with you so you can read them whenever you are going through a difficult time.

....

....

....

....

....

....

....

"If you want to have what you've never had,
you have to do what you've never done."

*Congratulations for working on Step Six! You are begin-
ning to prepare to change. If you notice your old ways and
thoughts resurfacing, go back and review the lessons you
learned in this Step.*

Become Your Best Self

DAY 186 TO DAY 215

.

Prepare for Transformation

Step Seven: "Humbly asked Him to remove our shortcomings."

By the time you start work on Step Seven, you have already begun to transform. It is painful to look at the way your addiction affected others. It is shameful and scary to honestly acknowledge what you did during active addiction. You may have done everything you could to block those memories, which only drove you deeper into drug use.

Now that you are free from the haze of drug use, you are more able to feel loved, protected, and guided by your Higher Power. Surely a Power who would do this for you does not consider you unlovable or unworthy. When you are working Steps Six and Seven, don't focus on whether or not your defects have been removed—that's your Higher Power's job. Everyone has character flaws that re-emerge despite their best efforts. This means that you are human. You are responsible for making a true effort to live a life that is better for you and the world around you. Focus on what you need to do to let your Higher Power go to work.

Meditate and try to envision the person you want to be. What changes do you need to make to become this person? Discuss your goals with your sponsor and ask him or her to hold you accountable for achieving them.

....

....

....

....

....

....

"The new life can't be built in a day. We have to take the program slowly,
a little at a time."
—*Twenty-Four Hours a Day,* January 18

Continue to Practice Willingness

Positive thinking can strengthen your willingness. Growth and change are not possible without willingness, which means you have to accept change before it can occur. Without a willingness to change, you remain stuck in your past limitations, illusions, and habits. Although willingness is not a guarantee that everything will turn out the way you want, you need to trust that your Higher Power knows best.

If you don't let go of self-will, you can't let go of past behaviors and beliefs. Page 76 in *Alcoholics Anonymous* suggests that you ask your Higher Power for courage as you continue to hand things over. Write a brief prayer to your Higher Power asking for guidance, strength, and faith as you keep letting go and letting God.

"Faith is taking the first step, even when you don't see the whole staircase."
—Martin Luther King Jr.

Continue to Build Relationships

Friends and family are mirrors that reflect who you are. Someone once said, "A blessed thing it is for any man or woman to have a friend, one human soul whom we can trust utterly, who knows the best and worst of us, and who loves us in spite of our faults." Think about that saying and answer these questions:

- Do you have any friends like the one described in the quote? Who are they?
- Are you this type of friend for anyone?
- How would you describe the difference between a friend and an acquaintance?
- Where can you make some new acquaintances who might become friends like this?
- What behaviors do you need to change to have more honest, trusting relationships?

"Friendship requires a mutual and equal bond of respect, trust,
and vulnerability that encourages healthy growth and acceptance."

Create a Seventh Step Prayer

The Little Red Book describes prayer as the "highest type of mental energy" for those in recovery. In prayer or meditation, you ask for your Higher Power's guidance; you give thanks for your recovery; and the very act of praying or meditating helps you stay clean and sober.

Asking your Higher Power for help is the most important part of Step Seven. Read the Seventh Step prayer on page 76 in *Alcoholics Anonymous.* When you pray this prayer, you humbly admit you don't have all the answers, and you ask that any barriers that block you from your Higher Power or prevent you from helping others be removed.

Using your own words, rewrite the Seventh Step prayer in a way that feels right for you. It doesn't matter how you ask for help—only that you do ask.

....

....

....

....

....

....

....

....

"A divine type of surgery is suggested by Steps Six and Seven. Humble prayer becomes the spiritual scalpel with which our Higher Power cuts the damaged portions from our sick personalities. Complete surrender to our Higher Power's will assures us a painless, successful operation."
—Adapted from *The Little Red Book*

Live with Humility

Humility is not humiliation or shame. Being *humble* means being teachable. With humility, you embrace "humanness" and accept yourself and others as being human. Humble beings realize they will never be perfect, but when they reach out, accept help, and offer it in return, they can be happier and live in community with other imperfect beings.

Describe what humility means to you. Can you remember a specific situation when you practiced or experienced great humility? What did you learn from this experience?

....

....

....

....

....

....

....

....

....

....

....

....

"Humility is not thinking less of yourself. It is thinking of yourself less."

Keep Working Step Seven

You don't get to control which of your character defects are removed or when this happens. You've put this process in your Higher Power's hands. You can help the process along by taking the appropriate action when you are guided to do so. For example, if you've prayed to your Higher Power to remove your out-of-control anger, you may want to seek help in therapy or attend anger-management classes.

Make a commitment to work on Step Seven by asking yourself the following questions:

- What is one character strength I can put into action for the next seven days?
- What is a character defect I can ask my Higher Power to remove?

"Surrender of our defects to a Higher Power is not the spiritless act of a defeatist; it is the intelligent act of an alcoholic who replaces fear and weakness with spiritual courage, understanding, strength, and contented sobriety."
—The Little Red Book

Embrace the Fellowship

Friendship is the best antidote to the loneliness and isolation of active addiction. The fellowship you can experience in Twelve Step recovery groups will change your life, if you let it. When you go to meetings, listen to others share the experiences, the hopes, and the strength they've found in recovery. They understand your challenges because they're addicts themselves. Most are nonjudgmental and more than willing to help newcomers learn, so consider talking to other Twelve Step members if you have questions about any aspect of recovery.

Sometimes your Higher Power uses other people to speak to you and help you, so reach out when you are comfortable doing so. In time, you will be able to help others as they have helped you. But you have to join the fellowship and go to meetings for that to happen.

Go to a Twelve Step meeting this week and listen to what others say about their experiences. Was anything said in the meeting that you relate to or can put into action? What can you do to make tomorrow better than today?

....

....

....

....

....

....

....

....

"The way of A.A. is the way of fellowship."
—*Twenty-Four Hours a Day,* December 9

Forgive to Be Free

Forgiveness is a choice, not a feeling. Forgiveness helps *you* let go of hurt and anger—it may or may not help others. It is a process that frees you to live life more fully. Forgiving is not forgetting, excusing, reconciling, or being weak. As one person put it, "Forgiveness was one of the hardest things in recovery for me, but now it means to let go and not to let the people who hurt me keep me locked to them with anger."

Practice forgiveness by writing a few practice letters that you will not send. For example:

Dear _____
I am angry that _____
I am sad that _____
I am afraid that _____
I am sorry that _____
Thanks for listening.
From _____

Next, write the response you'd like to hear from the other person. Then write a letter of forgiveness to that person accepting the apology and letting the issue go. Remember, don't send these forgiveness letters. They are meant to help you let go and be free from hurt. You don't need anyone else in order to achieve this freedom.

"When you forgive, you in no way change the past—
but you sure do change the future."
—Bernard Meltzer

Practice Being a True Friend

You may be worried that you don't know how to be a good friend. In the past, some of your friendships may have been built around drugs, parties, or lies. You can develop healthy friendships by doing the following:

- Promptly admit when you are wrong.
- Be honest with yourself and others.
- Talk openly about your recovery.
- Express your feelings.
- Help others even when it isn't convenient.
- Treat others the way you would like to be treated yourself.

Write about the traits you admire in someone you feel is a positive and healthy person. Think about the characteristics you would like to see in yourself and in your friends.

....

....

....

....

....

....

....

....

"When a friend is in trouble, don't annoy him by asking if there is anything you can do. Think up something appropriate and do it."
—Edgar Watson Howe

Practice Positive Thinking

Usually, addicts are their own worst enemies and critics. When you practice being more positive with others, remember to be more loving toward yourself as well. Attitude shifts begin from within, and it's difficult to see the positive in the world if you're looking through weary eyes that reflect low self-esteem or self-hatred.

Take a minute and quickly list any negative thoughts you've had about yourself recently. For every negative thought, write down two positive statements about yourself. Do you feel your attitude shift?

"Your own mind is a sacred enclosure into which nothing harmful can enter except by your permission."
—Ralph Waldo Emerson

Learn about Making Amends

To "amend" means to make better or to improve. Amends are much more than apologies; they are further expressions of our intention to change. Amends are an opportunity to acknowledge and sometimes make up for past wrongs. Most addicts know about shallow apologies; they got used to muttering a flippant "I'm sorry" when their addictive behavior got them in trouble. Amends are richer because they help release the baggage of the past and open the door to more honest and meaningful relationships. Amends are a shining gift to both the person making them and the person receiving them.

You've already made big changes, and you may already have experienced the humility that comes from facing the truth about yourself. But there is still past wreckage to clear so you can get on equal footing with others. Making amends is a choice to live honestly so you can face each new day clean and ready to move ahead.

Review your list of people you've harmed and describe why you need to make amends.

....

....

....

....

....

....

....

....

"No amend should be made that is not preceded by prayer."
—*The Little Red Book*

Practice Affirmations

Affirmations are positive and empowering statements about the ways you want to think, feel, and behave. They can change negative self-talk into a more loving and positive internal dialogue, helping you feel deserving and confident instead of guilt-ridden and shameful. Affirmations are not a substitute for reality; they are a way to tap into your best self: that inner strength that may have been overshadowed by the grip of addiction.

In the early stages of recovery, you spend a lot of time focusing on patterns of compulsion, denial, and self-destructive behavior. Affirmations are a way to assert that you are ready to celebrate your wonderfulness as well.

Start by paying attention to your negative self-talk. Write down those dark messages on a piece of paper and throw it away. Now, in the space below, write five positive statements such as "I, _____, am a good and loving person." There is power in attaching your name to the desired quality. Read the affirmations out loud. Celebrate yourself!

....

....

....

....

....

....

....

"Human beings, by changing the inner attitudes of their minds,
can change the outer aspects of their lives."
—William James

Establish Healthy Boundaries

Do you take care of others at the expense of taking care of yourself? Do you often feel like a martyr or feel a low sense of self-worth? If so, you may be in a codependent relationship—obsessed with controlling someone else's behavior. Some other major symptoms of codependency are

- denial
- overreacting or not reacting at all
- seeking approval
- substance abuse
- fear of abandonment
- becoming overly vigilant

You are as powerless over others as you are over your addiction. Establish healthy boundaries by learning when to say no and setting limits on what you will and won't do for others. Honor yourself and your recovery by not allowing anyone to physically or verbally abuse you. Make sure you don't take responsibility for rescuing others from the consequences of their own behaviors, including addictive behaviors. Don't let anger—yours or others'—control your life. Concentrate on what you need to do for yourself and your recovery.

Describe any codependent thoughts or behaviors you have. Are you afraid that someone you count on will abandon you? Do you have trouble enjoying time away from your spouse or partner? Do you compromise too much of your own needs, goals, and dreams in order to accommodate another person? How can you establish healthier boundaries?

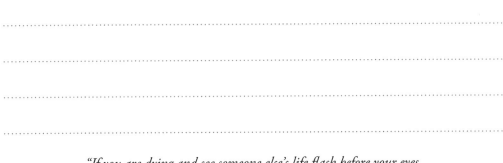

"If you are dying and see someone else's life flash before your eyes,
you might be codependent."

Examine Your Attitudes

Certain attitudes—grandiosity, perfectionism, rigid thinking, blame, shame, control, pessimism, hopelessness, isolation, self-pity, impatience, rationalization, resentment, anger—are red flags for relapse. They drain your energy and push healthy relationships away, leaving you alone and isolated.

An attitude of trust—in yourself, in others, and in your Higher Power—combats negative attitudes and solidifies recovery. A spiritual openness is also required to strengthen your resolve to abstain and to grow in recovery. Awareness and appreciation of the present moment will help you sort out what is real and what is "stinking thinking." Finally, an attitude of humility allows you to question, listen, learn, admit, assert, and clarify when you face challenging situations in your life.

Which negative attitudes are you trying to let go of? Which positive attitudes can replace them? Can you humbly admit mistakes and ask for help in letting go of harmful attitudes?

....

....

....

....

....

....

....

....

*"The calm and sane mind sees spiritual things as the true realities
and material things as only temporary and fleeting."*
—*Twenty-Four Hours a Day,* June 21

Evaluate Your Emotions

Consider Nicholas's story: "Even though I was nearing the one-year mark of recovery, I still felt anger, grief, resentment, and loneliness. I needed to find a healthy way to manage these emotions and make them a normal part of my life. My sponsor told me this struggle is common and reminded me to take it one day at a time."

At this point in recovery, like Nicholas, you may be wondering whether your feelings are normal. It is common to still have a need for drama, be hanging on to anger and resentment, feel loneliness, and be dealing with grief. Remember that feelings come and go and that they may not reflect the truth.

Continue to identify and acknowledge your feelings. Describe the feelings that are currently getting in the way of your recovery. Describe the feelings that are feeding your recovery. Make a commitment to talk to your sponsor each week about your emotions.

"I tell myself, 'I won't worry about my whole life, I'll just focus on dealing with these emotions today,' and that gets me by."

Watch Out for Blaming

On pages 216–218 in *Alcoholics Anonymous,* a recovering addict talks about how he kept finding excuses to drink. His wife and children caused him problems. His finances were in turmoil. Everyone annoyed him. He was angry and felt like God abandoned him, so he began to play God by trying to control others. But time and time again, the Twelve Step lessons and the recovery fellowship saved him and his sobriety.

There are always things and people to blame for your misfortunes, but playing the blame game is a dangerous activity that can lead to a relapse. Recovery is about accepting responsibility. It's about realizing that no excuse is worth a return to a life of active addiction.

Have you been thinking of excuses to justify using alcohol or other drugs? Are you blaming others for your difficulties? Describe some of these situations and list some ways you can avoid playing the blame game.

....

....

....

....

....

....

....

....

....

"To find a fault is easy; to do better may be difficult."
—Plutarch

Actualize Your Recovery Goals

Daydream a little and brainstorm your ideas for a rewarding and fulfilling life. There are no right or wrong answers, so don't censor yourself. Find a quiet time and place to relax, breathe deeply, and answer the following questions:

- If you could create a wonderful, but realistic, sober life for yourself—a life not defined by addiction—what would it be like?
- Where do you want to be a year from now?
- Is there anything you could do now to make these things happen?

"Each day I practice seeing myself as the person I am becoming—
not as the person I was."

Keep Avoiding Triggers

To be abstinent is to be free from mood-altering substances—not just your substance of choice. The dangers of "just one" are well known by those who know that it will start a chain reaction as your body attempts to capture its past euphoria.

Sobriety translates into physical, emotional, mental, and spiritual freedom. Your body has a chance to heal when you are abstinent, and as you grow stronger in recovery, your mind and spirit heal as well. To remain abstinent, continue to avoid environmental and emotional triggers that lead to drug use. Participate in healthy alternative behaviors when you experience cravings, and remind yourself that your goal is to remain abstinent from *all* substances. Go to meetings, and contact your sponsor and recovery friends whenever you feel the urge to use.

Review the triggers that threaten your abstinence. Do you have any new triggers? What positive steps can you take to honor and reinforce your abstinence?

....

....

....

....

....

....

....

....

"We all come to A.A. to get sober, and we stay to help others get sober.
We are looking for sobriety first, last, and all the time."
—*Twenty-Four Hours a Day,* November 27

Practice Acceptance

In friendship, it's very important to accept others as they are. Remembering the following will help you learn acceptance:

- You can only change yourself. Focus on improving yourself instead of controlling and changing others.
- Be at peace with others by accepting them where they are right now.
- Look for the good in others and focus on their positive traits.
- Celebrate differences instead of wanting others to be just like you.
- Don't complain about others or discount them. God created everyone unique with value and purpose.
- Allow others—and yourself—to be less than perfect.
- Allow others to live their own lives, and don't assume that you know better than they do.
- Get your life's meaning and purpose from your Higher Power, not from your friends.

Write about how you could be more accepting in one of your closest relationships. Then create a plan for improving that relationship.

....

....

....

....

....

....

....

....

"ABC = Accept, Believe, Change"

Manage Grief

When you entered recovery, you gave up the drug use around which your life revolved. Today, you choose to face the world without drugs to numb or mask your pain. Right now you may be dealing with some tough emotions. Active addiction may have caused you to become alienated from your family members and friends. Your self-worth may have plummeted to new lows.

With any of these losses comes grief, and a big part of recovery is giving yourself permission to embrace and honor grief as part of your growth process. Acknowledge it. Talk about it. Write about it. Allow yourself to feel grief without trying to fight it or fix it. Right now you may not be able to imagine a tomorrow that is better than today, but remember that grief is a temporary emotion that will pass with time.

List some things you've lost as a result of your addiction. Talk about your feelings of loss with someone in recovery. Does facing your grief help you begin to let it go?

"Give sorrow words; the grief that does not speak
whispers the o'er-fraught heart and bids it break."
—William Shakespeare

Practice the Serenity Prayer

You are continuing to evolve, but there are probably a few things you are still trying to control or change. Practice the Serenity Prayer (see Day 17) every day, and keep reminding yourself that there are only two types of problems: those you have the power to do something about and those over which only your Higher Power has control. When you accept that there are people, places, and things you cannot change, you can move on to those areas where your efforts can improve the situation. When you seek the courage to change the things you can, you draw upon your inner strength and your Higher Power's guidance to deal with the problems of life without falling back to drug use.

What are some things you cannot change, but wish you could change? What are some things you can change, but are afraid to change?

....

....

....

....

....

....

....

....

....

*"There's a time to make things happen, and a time to let things happen.
I pray that I will know the difference."*

Take Charge of Finances

Much of recovery is about creating balance in all aspects of your life. Like many people in the first year of recovery, you may still have financial problems that are a consequence of your drug use. Your Step Five work may have required you to pay some debts. But it's tough to make financial amends when you are having difficulty making ends meet. Remember that recovery involves asking for help. Start by talking with your sponsor about mending any lingering financial damage that you may be experiencing. If you need professional help with your finances, consider contacting the National Foundation for Credit Counseling (800-388-2227 or www.debtadvice.org): a network of nonprofit agencies that provides free or low-cost consumer counseling and education on budgeting, money management, debt reduction, and credit.

Describe the ways drug use has affected your financial condition. What steps can you take today to begin mending the damage? Imagine a life where money worries don't cause you fear. What does this life look like? Ask your Higher Power for help and guidance.

"They say that members of A.A. have paid the highest initiation fee of any club members in the world, because we've wasted so much money on liquor."
—*Twenty-Four Hours a Day,* January 29

Return the Holidays to a Spiritual Base

Many addicts are tempted to have "just one" drink during celebrations and holidays. Protect your recovery by going to an extra meeting or two, and create a plan that allows you to enjoy celebrations safely. You may want to take a sober friend along, or arrange a ride home if you need to leave the event suddenly. Make sure you let your sponsor know if you will attend a celebration that might expose you to triggers.

Think about ways you can return holidays and celebrations to a spiritual base. Instead of attending a beer-and-brats picnic on July 4, celebrate your independence from alcohol by doing something special with a friend in recovery. Honor the gift of recovery at Christmas or Hanukkah by serving meals at a shelter or wrapping presents for an elderly person. Create your own celebrations and thank your Higher Power for all the holy days that recovery brings.

List the holidays and celebrations that are coming up. Think of ways you can honor your recovery during each one.

....

....

....

....

....

....

....

....

"The holiest of all holidays are those kept by ourselves in silence and apart;
the secret anniversaries of the heart."
—Henry Wadsworth Longfellow

Continue to Be Patient

When you are working the Twelve Step program, be patient with yourself as well as with the process. It's not unusual to feel frustrated when thinking about the future of your recovery or when trying to meditate without a wandering mind. Everyone finds these things challenging. But eventually you'll have to face it: you aren't in charge. This means that "you are where you are, and it takes as long as it takes." If you're feeling impatient, tell your sponsor or talk about it in a meeting. Tell your Higher Power too, and ask for the ability to be patient with yourself. Just as you accept others, accept yourself as a work in progress.

Describe some recent times when you were impatient and how it affected you. How could you have relaxed and enjoyed life more by letting go of control and expecting instant gratification?

....

....

....

....

....

....

....

....

....

"Patience is the companion of wisdom."
—Saint Augustine

Keep Practicing Positive Affirmations

It may feel awkward at first—even a little fake—to say positive affirmations out loud. But in time, with practice, you will begin to believe the encouraging words you are telling yourself. Affirmations are another way to "act as if." When you act as if, you pretend you know what you're doing even when you aren't sure of yourself. You practice a behavior, an action, or a reaction until it becomes familiar.

Write down some loving, empowering affirmations for yourself. For example, "I am a beautiful person who is perfect just as I am today" or "I am a good person and I deserve to be happy."

Set a routine each day to read these affirmations. Look yourself in the mirror and believe them as you say them out loud. Soon, affirmations create a self-fulfilling prophecy that creates more positive energy in your life. Try it.

....

....

....

....

....

....

....

....

....

"Every morning I ask my Higher Power to reset my negative to positive."

Discover Your True Friends

How do you know whether someone is a good friend for you? Ask yourself the following questions about your friends:

- Do they support my recovery and help me to stay sober?
- Are they fun, funny, and interesting?
- Do they encourage me to grow as a person?
- Do they challenge me to make the changes I need to make?
- Do they treat me in a respectful, loving way?
- Can I share my feelings with them?
- Do they give me space when I need it and ask for it?
- Are they needy, possessive, or one-sided?

You get to choose how you interact with others. Establish healthy boundaries and spend less time—or no time at all—with people who don't support your sobriety or who don't help you grow as a person.

Make a list of all your friends, and for each one, answer the questions posed above. Decide which ones support your recovery. Staying sober comes first, so try not to feel guilty if someone doesn't make the cut.

....

....

....

....

....

....

"A true friend is one who walks in when the rest of the world walks out."

Acknowledge Failures with Grace

Admitting your failures helps you face the negative emotions that block recovery, such as shame, guilt, and remorse. This admission is an integral part of working an honest program filled with humility, openness, and willingness. Addicts are a host of contradictions. You may have become an expert at projecting wholeness when you felt empty or acting arrogant when you felt insecure. Acknowledging your failures helps you accept yourself with total honesty. No one is perfect; the danger comes when you're trying to hide your imperfections from others or when you're not learning from past mistakes.

Assess your ability to admit failure by answering these questions:

- Can you admit to yourself and others when you have made a mistake?
- Can you apologize for mistakes without shaming yourself?
- Can you take active steps to right wrongs made by the mistake?

....

....

....

....

....

....

....

....

....

"There are no losers in recovery."

Set Healthy Boundaries

Maintaining appropriate boundaries is key to sobriety. Most people will respect your boundaries if you let them know what they are. If you have trouble saying no, or change your behavior to pacify others, or focus on others' needs instead of your own, you may need to set boundaries. The goal of healthy boundaries is to enrich relationships—not isolate you. With healthy boundaries, you have the right to

- say no if your rights or space are invaded
- take care of yourself
- claim your own identity
- explore your own interests
- be respected, and protect your space and rights
- claim and express your feelings

Use "I" statements to rewrite the list of healthy boundaries in your own words (for example, "I have the right to . . ."). Talk with your sponsor or a recovery friend about how you might set better boundaries.

....

....

....

....

....

....

"Appropriate boundaries are the way you differentiate yourself from others;
they protect and preserve your individuality and help keep your self-esteem intact."

Understand Your Communication Style

Many people struggle with being too passive or too aggressive. If you are too passive, you may deny yourself many of your rights. You may avoid expressing feelings, remain hurt and anxious, give up your right to choose, or fail to reach your goals. If you are too aggressive, you might find that you minimize others or deny others' rights.

Once you understand your communication style, you can make adjustments that will improve your ability to connect with others. If you don't listen well, make a commitment to practice silence and don't interrupt others. If you are too loud or soft-spoken, try to adjust the volume of your voice. Do you put others first or last? Practice ways to balance everyone's needs and make sure they are recognized and respected.

Describe your communication style. What things can you do to achieve a better balance?

....

....

....

....

....

....

....

....

....

....

"We have two ears and one mouth so that we can listen twice as much as we speak."
—Epictetus

Forgive Others

When you were using, it's likely that you caused harm to others. You might have acted out in anger and said things you regret, or you might have neglected your family and friends.

You are almost ready to work Step Eight, where you start to make amends for the harms you have caused. At the same time, you may expect others to take responsibility for their part in a harmful situation. Be aware that just because you are ready to make amends, it doesn't mean the other person is ready. Try to stay focused on cleaning up "your side of the street" and realize that other people may not be ready to accept or acknowledge harms they have caused. In fact, they may be as "spiritually sick" as you were when you used alcohol and other drugs.

Read pages 66–67 in *Alcoholics Anonymous* to learn how to forgive the people who have wronged you by practicing the tolerance, pity, and patience you would cheerfully grant a sick friend. Describe a person you are having trouble forgiving. Talk to your sponsor about what is bothering you and ask for ideas on how to resolve the situation.

....

....

....

....

....

....

....

....

"By forgiving others, I learn to forgive myself."

Congratulations for working on Step Seven! You are beginning to become your best self. If you notice your old ways and thoughts resurfacing, go back and review the lessons you learned in this Step.

Act with Accountability

DAY 216 TO DAY 245

Honor Yourself with Honesty

Step Eight: "Made a list of all persons we had harmed, and became willing to make amends to them all."

If Steps Four through Seven are about "coming clean," Steps Eight and Nine are about "cleaning up." To recover, you need to put your life in order and right the wrongs you have done. Cleaning up your messes—whether you made them because of carelessness, fear, anger, jealousy, pride, or some other character defect—is part of changing an unmanageable life into one guided by the will of your Higher Power.

If you did a thorough Step Four inventory, you gained an understanding of "self-will run riot," as the Big Book says. In Step Eight, you list specific people you have harmed and become willing to think and act differently.

To begin Step Eight, review your inventory, then list the names of people you feel you have harmed. Talk to your sponsor or recovery group if you are unsure whom to include.

"It is not difficult to list the people who suffered because we drank.
Our real problem is to arrive at a state of mind that concedes
the damage we have done and embraces a sincere willingness to amend it."
—*The Little Red Book*

Let Go of Unhealthy Pride

There are two sides to the pride coin: (1) healthy pride that creates self-respect, confidence, and healthy self-esteem and (2) unhealthy pride that accompanies an inflated sense of ego. Healthy pride feeds your recovery by bolstering your sense of achievement and self-worth. Unhealthy pride keeps you from experiencing the humility necessary to honestly face your character defects and ask for help.

Recovery groups are filled with people who have battled overconfidence, pride, and overreliance on self-will. Sharing your feelings and talking with them will help you regain a sense of humor and belonging.

Describe times when you have felt or exhibited a healthy sense of pride. How does healthy pride bolster your recovery? Who can you talk to when you are feeling unhealthy pride?

"[Humility is] freedom from false pride and arrogance."
—*The Little Red Book*

Keep Improving Social Skills

No one is born with great social skills. They develop these skills by watching others and modeling what they see. You can do the same thing. From your circle of friends, family, and recovery group members, choose someone whose social skills you admire. Observe that person closely and notice what he or she does to make you feel welcome. Is there a smile, a handshake, a greeting by name, or a little joke?

Practice those same behaviors. Care enough to remember names and personal details, and ask about these things at your next meeting. Extend your hand to shake. Imagine what a person might need and ask to provide it, whether it's a place to sit or a cup of coffee.

List some things you can do at your next meeting to connect with others.

"Be sincere; be brief; be seated."
—Franklin Delano Roosevelt

Make Recovery a Habit

As a recovering addict, you know all about bad habits. Recovery is about replacing the negative habits of addiction with the healthy habits of the Twelve Step spiritual program. These are the seven habits of successful sobriety:

1. Forget willpower and embrace your Higher Power. Accept that addiction is a disease and abstinence is the only solution.
2. Use the problem-solving skills you are learning in recovery to stabilize your emotions.
3. Learn to identify and manage stress.
4. Build a sobriety-based lifestyle by engaging in healthy recreation with sober friends.
5. Learn to let go of self-defeating behaviors.
6. Be prepared for the lifelong process of continued personal growth and development.
7. Don't get lazy with recovery. It takes focus to abstain for a lifetime.

Review this list of habits. Describe how well you're practicing each at this point in your recovery.

....

....

....

....

....

....

....

"It's kind of fun to do the impossible."
—Walt Disney

Remove Self-Pity

Relief from self-pity is one of the promises of sobriety. But how is that promise fulfilled? Start by talking to your sponsor or a friend in recovery about how he or she manages destructive thoughts. Observe for yourself when you're indulging in the luxury of self-pity. Seek your Higher Power's help in removing this defect of character.

When you feel your misfortunes are taking up all of your thoughts, try helping someone else with a problem they're having. Listen attentively to a friend who's upset about something. Thank your Higher Power for your sobriety, and cultivate an attitude of gratitude.

If self-pity creeps in despite your best efforts, meditate on your thoughts and then describe them in writing. Are they true statements or created fears? You may also want to share your thoughts with people who have more experience in recovery than you do, such as your sponsor or recovery support group.

....

....

....

....

....

....

....

....

"Self-pity is our worst enemy and if we yield to it,
we can never do anything wise in this world."
—Helen Keller

Practice Trust

Look back on the last couple of weeks. Are you trusting others more? Sometimes incidents in your past make it hard for you to open yourself up to possible hurt or rejection. You might often feel anxious and suspicious of others. If you find it hard to trust new people, counseling or group therapy might be helpful. In group therapy, you can hear other people's stories and identify with them. You can learn to be sympathetic to their struggles and get comfortable with admitting your own. You can also learn stress-management techniques like meditation or breathing exercises so you aren't so anxious around others.

Create a scale of 1 to 10 (10 being "trust absolutely"), and rate your level of trust with your friends, family, and people in your Twelve Step meeting. If you score consistently on the low end of the trust scale, consider counseling or group therapy.

....

....

....

....

....

....

....

....

....

"One must be fond of people and trust them if one is not to make a mess of life."
—E. M. Forster

Prepare to Make Amends

You have already begun your list of people to whom you need to make amends. Putting these names in writing helps you gain clarity about the harm you have caused, and it keeps you honest. It is too easy to be selective in your memories when you begin the process of making amends, but once a name is written down, it is real, and you know you must attend to the matter sooner or later.

When you develop your list, don't worry about making the actual amends or the consequences of making them. You don't have to make amends yet; that happens in Step Nine. When that time comes, trust that you will be guided to do what you must do.

For now, review your list of people and reasons for making amends. Prioritize your amends using four categories: now, later, maybe later, and never. Here again, ask for help from your sponsor or group if you need it.

....

....

....

....

....

....

....

....

....

"We cannot hate and make amends at the same time."
—*The Little Red Book*

Avoid Workaholism

Going back to work in early recovery can be challenging, but if you lean on your recovery network and your Higher Power for support, the challenge is made easier. At first, you may be tempted to try to make up for lost time by working too hard and too much. You can avoid "workaholism" when you remember to

- fiercely guard your time for recovery-related activities like Twelve Step meetings and working the Steps, remembering always that recovery is your number-one priority
- take a five-minute break every hour to read a meditation, get a drink of water, or greet a co-worker
- pick one important task at a time to work on, then move to the next one, checking off each completed task as a motivation to keep going
- make sure to exercise, meditate, connect with nature, journal, laugh, and/or talk with a friend every day in order to maintain balance

Write down three specific things you can do today to avoid workaholism.

....

....

....

....

....

....

....

"First things first."

Remember "Easy Does It"

Living sober and working hard on your spiritual recovery program can seem pretty intense at times. In the beginning, you may be tempted to delve into recovery in a compulsive way that exhausts you and actually threatens your sobriety. Let go of trying to fix all the problems in the world, and always remember that using drugs and alcohol won't solve anything either. Addicts get used to doing everything to excess, so when they enter recovery, they need to slow down and take it easy.

Read page 357 in *Alcoholics Anonymous.* Describe some of the ways you can take it easy this week.

....

....

....

....

....

....

....

....

....

"You must be *before you can* do. *To accomplish much, be much . . .*
Quiet times of communion with the Higher Power
are good preparation for creative action."
—*Twenty-Four Hours a Day,* May 2

Keep Working Step Eight

In Step Eight, you welcome compassion into your life, and in Step Nine, you will put that compassion into action. Read pages 76–84 in *Alcoholics Anonymous,* and review your list of the people you have harmed. If you haven't started a list yet, do it now. This list should be written or typed, and you may want to divide your paper into four columns as follows:

- friends you have harmed and how
- family members you have harmed and how
- those you have harmed financially
- those you have harmed who are no longer living

Review your list and describe how this process feels. Are you facing any tough emotions that are holding you back from making amends? Discuss your list with your sponsor or a recovery friend.

....

....

....

....

....

....

....

....

"I didn't make amends to punish myself; I did it to move beyond
the shame, guilt, and hopelessness that were holding me back.
Now I can face each day clean and ready to move ahead."

Handle Challenging Feelings

When you describe your problems and emotions in a journal, you may discover the source of your feelings. You might see that your feelings are based on irrational beliefs or fears. If you see a trend in your emotions, such as always feeling sad, you may want to seek outside help.

Know that it is okay to feel whatever you feel, but you should think about your feelings before you react to them. This doesn't mean to ignore your feelings. Stuffing or ignoring your feelings can result in physical illness, stress, overeating, or other difficulties. Feelings don't go away, so it's best to deal with them when they arise.

Write down words that describe how you are feeling right now. Were there other times this week when you experienced strong feelings? Name those feelings. Think about your life these past few years and name one or two feelings you experienced frequently. Are there a couple of feelings you'd like to feel less often?

....

....

....

....

....

....

....

....

....

....

"If you want to keep feeling the way you are feeling, keep doing what you are doing."

Keep an Eye on Stress

As a recovering person, you are especially vulnerable to stress. When you feel overwhelmed, you may be tempted to seek a quick, reliable solution by using drugs.

Stressful situations include anything that makes you feel physically ill, hungry, tired, shameful, inadequate, lonely, hopeless, angry, or resentful. What are some of the high-stress areas that you face at this point in your life? List a few situations or people that make you feel stressed. Work with your sponsor, recovery group, and family to develop a stress-management plan. Your plan may be as simple as deciding not to associate with certain people or not to attend certain events. It might also mean letting go of things you cannot change. Make the Serenity Prayer part of your daily routine. Use it to sort out what is really important and identify things you can let go of.

"God, grant me the serenity to accept the things I cannot change, the courage to change the things I can, and the wisdom to know the difference."
—Serenity Prayer

Find a Physician

If you don't already have a physician who understands addiction and recovery, find one before an urgent health problem arises. Be up front with your physician about your addiction. If your physician is aware of your addiction, he or she can prescribe or recommend appropriate medications that won't threaten your recovery. Ask the following questions about a current or potential physician:

- Does the physician agree that addiction is a chronic disease, and recovery is a lifelong process?
- Does the physician understand that addicts are as powerless over addiction as a diabetic is over diabetes—that no amount of willpower will remove either disease?
- Will the physician avoid prescribing potentially addictive medications whenever possible?

Do you have any fears that stop you from sharing your addiction with health care providers? If so, describe them here. Talk with your sponsor or recovery group to find ways to overcome your fears.

....

....

....

....

....

....

....

"My sobriety is more important than other people's opinions of me."

Overcome Denial

For addicts, denial occurs when they refuse to acknowledge the problems their addiction has caused. Denial can manifest itself as minimization, rationalization, justification, or blame, to name just a few. You might use denial to sidestep shameful, uncomfortable, or painful events or to lessen your deep feelings of fear, guilt, shame, anxiety, and inadequacy.

While denial happens within you, your friends and family often suffer from it too because they don't want to admit you have the lifelong disease of addiction. This denial can dilute your honesty and weaken the foundation of any amends you attempt to make.

Rigorous honesty is the best antidote for denial. Read page 328 in *Alcoholics Anonymous* about denial. Describe your patterns of denial and how you can focus on the truth. Try to identify one of the Twelve Steps that can help you break out of your habit of denial.

....

....

....

....

....

....

....

....

....

"Denial is not just a river in Egypt."

Overcome Barriers to Acceptance

Addiction is often described as a combination of two problems: the using problem and the thinking problem. The using problem includes the physical, while the thinking problem deals with roadblocks to acceptance, including

- conflict with those who do not behave as you might wish
- self-pity
- unmet expectations that cause anger or resentment
- a sense of loss that stirs up fear, blame, or loneliness
- relapse

You overcome these barriers by letting go of character defects that hold you back. You accept your powerlessness over others by realizing you can only change yourself.

List some of your barriers to acceptance. For each, list a character defect that is interfering with your ability to achieve the acceptance you desire.

....

....

....

....

....

....

....

....

....

"Just accept, don't expect."

Talk to Your Children about Recovery

You may not know what to say about your disease to your children, who may be acting as if everything is fine or acting aloof and withdrawn because they are holding on to their own anger and resentment. As a recovering addict, you might feel hypocritical when you talk to your children about issues of trust and the dangers of drug use. But your most important job as a parent is to honestly inform and protect your children. There are many resources available to help you teach your children about addiction and recovery. Ask your sponsor and recovery group to help you obtain materials if you can't find them.

Before you talk with your children, honestly examine your motives. Do you want to create a better relationship? Are you trying to keep them away from drugs or alcohol? Are you trying to relieve your own guilt? Write the answers to those questions. Then identify some positive things you would like to accomplish, such as reestablishing trust or reinforcing your love. Focus on the positive goals.

....

....

....

....

....

....

....

....

*"Those children who saw me drunk and were ashamed . . . have turned to me
in confidence and trust and have forgotten the past as best they could."*
—*Twenty-Four Hours a Day,* October 29

Uncover Your False Self

When you were actively addicted, you got used to wearing a mask to cover up what was really going on. Like other addicts, you developed a false self to avoid rejection and hide secrets. It's hard for addicts to believe they are lovable. They fear being taken advantage of if they show their true self or exhibit any weakness.

Have you found yourself thinking things like "If I showed you the real me, you probably wouldn't like me, so I'll try to be who I think you want me to be"? A major job of recovery is to unmask your false self in order to connect with your true self.

Read the story on pages 382–387 in *Alcoholics Anonymous*. Write down ways you expressed your false self and what your false traits accomplished, such as helping you appear confident to avoid rejection. Then think about who you truly are by focusing on your positive traits, such as being honest and hopeful. Which false traits are in conflict with your true traits? Which do you need to let go of?

....

....

....

....

....

....

....

....

....

"The greatest mistake you can make in life
is to be continually fearing you will make one."
—Elbert Hubbard

Rebuild Trust

Trust is the firm reliance on the integrity, ability, or character of another person or thing. It is a quality that may have gotten badly damaged during your addiction, and it takes some work to repair broken trust. You rebuild trust by becoming trustworthy, which means taking responsibility for your actions and being there for others. You become trustworthy by focusing on recovery, rather than on relationships, and by working the Steps with an open and honest heart.

Make a commitment to become more trustworthy by asking others what you could do to rebuild their trust. Maybe it's calling when you'll be late, listening attentively, or telling the truth. Take a minute to write down some ways you might rebuild trust.

....

....

....

....

....

....

....

....

....

....

"To trust, become trustworthy."

Deal with Mental Health Symptoms

It is common for addicts to also have an underlying mental health disorder, such as depression or anxiety. These disorders are not a reflection of personal weakness, lack of willpower, or poor moral character; they are a disease, like addiction. If you are diagnosed with depression, anxiety, bipolar disorder, or another disorder, remember that you are not responsible for the disease. You are, however, responsible for getting help. You don't have to suffer; there are effective treatments that can help you recover.

If you suspect you have a mental health disorder, seek a diagnosis from a qualified person such as a psychologist, psychiatrist, or other mental health professional who is experienced in Twelve Step recovery. If you treat your mental health disorder, you will greatly improve your success with sobriety.

Have you experienced thoughts of suicide or emotional difficulties that haven't lessened or that have grown worse since you began your recovery program? Describe these feelings. Talk to your sponsor and recovery group right away to get some names and phone numbers of qualified mental health professionals who are familiar with addiction and recovery.

"Mental illness is nothing to be ashamed of; but stigma and bias shame us all."
—Bill Clinton

Consider Counseling

Recovery is a lifelong journey, and a licensed counselor or therapist who understands addiction can help you address ongoing issues by

- teaching you to recognize and re-channel your urge to use alcohol or drugs
- supporting your abstinence
- holding you accountable and discussing relapses
- helping you identify potential relapse situations
- helping you develop healthy problem-solving strategies for stress, anger, and frustration
- supporting your Twelve Step involvement
- helping you develop a lifelong recovery plan
- helping you identify relapse triggers
- helping you improve your self-esteem

Counseling can also help you deal with anxiety, depression, and bipolar or other co-occurring disorders. If you have a co-occurring mental health disorder, follow your doctor's recommendations and seek support from your recovery group.

Trust your gut when you choose a therapist. An effective counselor is genuine, respectful of your questions and concerns, skilled, certain to involve you in your therapy program, and trustworthy. Describe your feelings about therapy, and if you think you could benefit from it, who you might choose as a qualified counselor.

....

....

....

....

....

....

"Recovery is a journey, not a destination."

Learn to Listen

Listening is more than hearing, and being a good listener is an important part of friendship. When you really listen, you focus on others so you understand not only what is being said but also how they are feeling. The following tips can help you become a more attentive listener:

- Show you are listening by maintaining eye contact, nodding your head, and saying things like "uh-huh" or "I understand."
- Paraphrase what the other person has said, and ask questions if you don't understand.
- Don't respond until the other person has finished talking. Interrupting is a sign that you aren't listening attentively.

Describe a time when you were really listened to and how that experience felt. Set a goal to really listen to someone at least once a day.

....

....

....

....

....

....

....

....

"Learn to listen, and listen to learn."

Examine Your Work Life

While you were in active addiction, it's likely that your work performance suffered. You may have been late to work or not shown up for work at all. In response, your co-workers and supervisors may have become confused, angry, or resentful. They may have even been fearful that you would hurt yourself or get fired. They may have also worried that they would be held responsible if they were caught covering up for you.

Many addicts have gotten caught up in the dishonesty of trying to keep everything looking good on the surface at work, while their addiction grows unchecked.

Read pages 136–150 in *Alcoholics Anonymous.* Describe how addiction has undermined your career and relationships with co-workers and supervisors. When have you been at fault or harmed others at work? What things do you appreciate and offer gratitude for at work?

"To some extent, we are all labeled by what we're able to achieve.
But more importantly, we are defined by what we attempt."
—Scott Tinley

Keep Managing Stress

When you were new to recovery, you discovered how vulnerable you are to certain situations, events, and people that repeatedly cause you stress. You learned to practice saying no to the stressful things you can eliminate. You learned how to make better choices by prioritizing and scheduling the stressful things that be cannot be avoided. Remember that stressful situations include anything that makes you feel physically ill, hungry, tired, shameful, inadequate, lonely, hopeless, angry, or resentful.

While you can't eliminate stress altogether, you can practice identifying and managing it when it arises—before it takes a physical toll or drives you into relapse. When someone pushes your buttons or something frustrates you, reduce and manage your stress by

- asking your Higher Power for wisdom
- calling a recovering friend for feedback
- giving yourself a short break, such as counting to ten or going for a walk and waiting for your emotions to cool

Describe how well you're managing stress. If you are having difficulty, which of the above strategies can you adopt right now to lessen your stress?

....

....

....

....

....

....

"There is more to life than increasing its speed."
—Mohandas Gandhi

Keep Letting Go of Resentments

Resentment grows from unresolved anger and the belief that you have been wronged, which can cause bitterness and rob you of joy, compassion, and happiness. Feelings of hatred and revenge can consume your thoughts and threaten your sobriety. You can't control what others do (or did), but you can control how you respond. If you hold on to resentments, you may use them as an excuse to justify using again. But no one can cause you to relapse—your sobriety is solely your responsibility.

To preserve your recovery, let go of resentments as soon as they start to build. Close your eyes and picture the person you resent bathed in compassion. If you can't do this, try some objectivity: the person you resent might be as sick as you were when you were using.

Write down a list of people you resent and describe what happed and how you feel about it. Write down how the resentment is harming you. Is it diminishing trust or causing rage? Brainstorm a few ways you could let go of this resentment, such as practicing forgiveness or meditation.

"Hanging on to resentment is like letting someone you can't stand
live rent-free in your head."

Keep Working the Twelve Steps

Working the Twelve Steps is like training for a marathon. You don't just wake up, lace up your shoes, and run twenty-six miles. You start out slowly. You complete short runs, build up your endurance, and then go the distance. To keep in shape after the race, you continue to exercise, and you always try to stretch first.

The Twelve Steps don't help people handle alcohol; they teach people how to handle sobriety. That is why addicts must work the Steps again and again. As you change and grow, your circumstances also change. The Twelve Steps are always there. They are a deep well from which you drink the wisdom to sustain you during life's challenges.

In your own words, describe what the Twelve Steps represent to you.

....

....

....

....

....

....

....

....

....

....

"No matter how far off the path we've stumbled,
we're no more than Twelve Steps away from the solution."

Practice Patience

Even instant gratification can take too long for addicts. When you were using, you may have impatiently sought the quickest high to escape your emotional pain. Like some addicts, you may have turned to drugs when drinking didn't get you high fast enough.

There's a reason for the slogan "Time takes time." You have to learn to be patient in order to succeed in recovery. You have to slow down, change your behavior, and take things one day at a time. You may not realize for years how getting sober is changing your life. Trust that you are making progress and growing spiritually every day that you stay sober and work the program. It happens slowly and subtly. If you rush it, it may not happen at all.

Look to your Higher Power for patience. Ask your sponsor and fellow addicts how they practice patience. Then list ten ways you can practice patience yourself.

....

....

....

....

....

....

....

....

....

"God give me patience—right now!"

Live It Up

Just because you are in recovery doesn't mean you can't have fun and enjoy each day of your new life. Consider this story from a heroin addict and alcoholic with two years in recovery: "I have had more fun since I got sober than I ever did when I was high. I used to get smashed almost every night and couldn't even remember what happened or if I even had fun at all. Now I have a 'home group'; we all go out for coffee after our meetings. We joke and laugh every time we hang out. I never laughed that much when I was drunk and high. We also go to AA dances, picnics, and retreats. I can always call someone from my home group and find something to do."

Now that you have had time to attend quite a few meetings, have you found a "home group" of people whose company you enjoy? If not, think about a few people you want to get to know better, and list their names here. After the next meeting, ask those people out for coffee. You could start your own coffee group or a movie or book club. Don't wait for someone else to do the work. Reach out and make connections with sober friends today.

"If you can't be funny, be interesting."
—Harold Ross

Tell Your Story

By this point in your recovery, you may have noticed that your outlook on life is constantly improving, even though you still have ups and downs. By working the Steps and going to meetings, you have begun to change how you think and how you respond to things in life.

Take time today to reflect on who you were when you were using, and think about how far you have come. Share your story with others at the next meeting. Telling your story helps you see the progress you have made. Believe it or not, your story will help others who might need some extra inspiration or hope.

What were you like when you were using? What was your life like? What happened to get you into recovery? What is your life like now? How have you changed?

"Use your imagination not to scare yourself to death but to inspire yourself to life."
—Adele Brookman

Keep Building Your Self-Esteem

Low self-esteem can undermine your best efforts to enjoy your life and actualize your goals. Negative self-messages can creep in and take away your power to achieve the things you want. You might find that when you try a new, challenging task that your old "critic" comes out and says, "You'll never be able to do that very well, so why waste your time?" The truth is that most of these negative self-messages just aren't true. They aren't based on any facts; they are only based on fear and a lack of acceptance for the normal process of learning. Nobody is perfect. Remember, you can't look forward to new growth unless you take some risks and try. You are only responsible for your effort, not the outcome.

Are you being held back by low-self-esteem? Are fears of failure or being less than perfect keeping you from trying something new? List at least three things that you are really good at or that you like about yourself. What new thing can you try today?

....

....

....

....

....

....

....

....

"You gain strength, courage and confidence by every experience
in which you really stop to look fear in the face. You are able to say to yourself,
'I have lived through this horror. I can take the next thing that comes along.'
You must do the thing you think you cannot do."
—Eleanor Roosevelt

Revisit Steps One Through Eight

By now, you should have built a firm foundation with the first eight Steps. If you feel reluctant to move forward, it may be that you haven't completed a previous Step thoroughly. Before you start Step Nine and start making amends, ask yourself the following questions:

- Have I admitted that I'm truly powerless over my addiction and that my life has become unmanageable (Step One)?
- Have I made a firm and real decision to turn my will and life over to my Higher Power (Steps Two and Three)?
- Have I been as honest as I can about how my addiction has harmed others (Steps Four and Five)?
- Have I asked my Higher Power to remove my character defects, and do I trust that this will happen (Steps Six and Seven)?
- Have I made a list of all the people I have harmed, and am I now willing to start making amends (Step Eight)?

If you can honestly answer yes to these questions, you are in a good position to do the meaningful work that Step Nine requires. If you answered no to any of them, talk to your sponsor or your group to figure out why you are stuck in the process.

....

....

....

....

....

....

....

"Is your program powered by willpower or by a Higher Power?"

Congratulations for working on Step Eight! You are begin-
ning to act with accountability. If you notice your old ways
and thoughts resurfacing, go back and review the lessons
you learned in this Step.

Grow Strong and True

DAY 246 TO DAY 275

Understand the Importance of Amends

Step Nine: "Made direct amends to such people wherever possible, except when to do so would injure them or others."

Step Nine is another call to action—a challenge to try to restore relationships and repair the harm that has been caused. You might resist this Step by denying you really hurt others. You might feel that others hurt you worse, or you might balk at doing something as uncomfortable as making amends. You cannot predict how others might react, but making amends is not always difficult or unpleasant. Often, the relief you feel at taking responsibility for your actions energizes you.

Working Step Nine is essential to recovery. You are usually rewarded by a lessening of guilt, shame, remorse, and fear after you make amends. Making amends feeds your recovery and increases your resolve to be abstinent.

Describe in your own words why you think you need to make amends. What do you think you'll gain by doing Step Nine?

....

....

....

....

....

....

....

....

"AA teaches us that to 'live and let live' is to safeguard our sobriety."
—*The Little Red Book*

Keep Practicing Humility

Humility is not about inadequacy or weakness. It's about accepting that you are human, and as such, you are both imperfect and wonderful. Humility requires honesty as you continue to let go of the need to feel superior to others or be right all the time. When you practice humility, you strive to let go of your character defects and embrace spiritual values.

Mother Teresa said, "If you are humble nothing can touch you, neither praise nor disgrace, because you know who you are. If you are blamed you will not be discouraged. If they call you a saint you will not put yourself on a pedestal." Respond to Mother Teresa's statement about humility by briefly describing what being humble means to you.

....

....

....

....

....

....

....

....

....

....

"If you do not tell the truth about yourself you cannot tell it about other people."
—Virginia Woolf

Learn a New Skill

Have you ever yearned to learn to play an instrument such as the piano or guitar? Have you ever thought about writing short stories, playing chess, or painting? Now that you're sober, a new world awaits you, filled with hobbies and adventures that are more fun (and safer) than using. Imagine hanging a painting that you created or performing a song on the guitar. The pride you can take in your accomplishments is a high you can't get from any substance.

List some things you've always wanted to try, perhaps drawing, painting, woodworking, writing, singing, or dancing. Brainstorm about where to go or whom to contact for more information. Check out community education in your area, or call a musician or artist friend for advice. Host a nonalcoholic jam session. The possibilities are endless.

"A ship that stays in the harbor is safe, but that's not what ships are for."

Keep Building Self-Esteem

Self-esteem is the opinion you have of yourself. It is made up of self-confidence and self-worth. Self-confidence is feeling good about what you *do* and feeling capable of doing things. Self-worth is feeling good about who you *are* and feeling lovable and worthwhile.

When you were using, you may have been very negative toward yourself. One way to break this habit is by changing the negative statements about yourself to positive ones. Instead of saying to yourself, "Nobody likes me," you could say, "I am a person that many people like." Instead of saying, "I never do anything right," you could say, "I have done many things right." Instead of saying, "I'll never get a good job," say, "I will get a good job."

Make a list of the negative things you tell yourself. For each, develop a positive statement to counter it. To reinforce the positive statements, read them before you go to bed at night and right when you wake up in the morning. Take a moment to realize that the negative things you say are really lies. The truth is that you really do many things right—and you will do more things right in the future.

....

....

....

....

....

....

....

....

"We obtain self-esteem by doing esteemable things."

Grow in Confidence

Self-confidence grows as you take on challenges and accomplish new things. It is gained through practice. For example, the more you work the Steps, the more confident you will become in your ability to work them. You can also grow self-confidence in relationships by being with people who support you and your recovery.

Make a list of the things you are really good at doing. Then make a list of the challenges you have taken on in recovery and how you felt after you faced these challenges. And last, list those who love you for who you are, not for what you do. How do these positive things and people help build your self-confidence?

....

....

....

....

....

....

....

....

....

....

"Believe in yourself! Have faith in your abilities! Without a humble but reasonable confidence in your own powers you cannot be successful or happy."
—Norman Vincent Peale

Learn about Depression

Depression is a disease that involves the body and mind. It affects how you eat and sleep, how you feel about yourself, and how you think. Depression is not the same as occasional sadness; it tends to be more prolonged and severe. Like addiction, depression is not a sign of personal weakness or something that can be "wished away."

If you suffer from chemical dependency and depression, you may have to be treated for both diseases at the same time in order to fully recover. If you think you suffer from depression, talk to your sponsor about your feelings and get a referral to a mental health professional in your area.

Describe how you experience any of the following symptoms in early recovery and how they affect your life, relationships, and thinking:

- ongoing sadness
- feelings of hopelessness
- feelings of guilt, worthlessness, or helplessness
- loss of interest in hobbies or activities
- fatigue
- difficulty concentrating or making decisions

- insomnia or oversleeping
- changes in appetite or weight
- restlessness or irritability
- persistent headaches, digestive disorders, or chronic pain
- thoughts of suicide

If you are feeling very positive, give thanks. Talk to your sponsor or a recovery friend about how you are feeling this week.

....

....

....

....

....

"I pray that I may strive for inward peace. I pray that I may not be seriously upset, no matter what happens around me."
—*Twenty-Four Hours a Day,* July 28

Make Direct Amends

Step Nine: "Made direct amends to such people wherever possible, except when to do so would injure them or others."

Step Nine requires you to make *direct* amends to those you've harmed. Whenever possible, you should meet the injured person face-to-face. If the person lives far away, you can telephone or write a letter. To be meaningful, amends should match the offense. For example, if you apologize to a friend for an unpaid debt but make no plans to repay it, your amends fall short of their intended goal. If you express regret to your partner for hurtful behavior but make no effort to control your anger, you are not making amends.

You may be reluctant to make amends to someone you've harmed who has also harmed you, but Step Nine asks you to take responsibility, not to judge. The important thing is not when you make amends, but whether you make amends. Pray to your Higher Power for guidance. If you still struggle, seek advice from your sponsor or group.

Be gentle with yourself and give yourself credit for the progress you have made. Write three affirmations that can help in making amends, such as "I am a loving person, capable of seeing my flaws."

....

....

....

....

....

....

"When you go to a person and say you are sorry, a load is off your chest
and often an enemy has been turned into a friend."
—Adapted from *Twenty-Four Hours a Day,* September 22

Get Creative If You Can't Make Direct Amends

Sometimes you can't make direct amends because a person has died or cannot be found. In these cases, you might want to write an unsent letter or donate time or money to a cause you know was close to that person's heart. You may want to help that person's family in some way. Remember, willingness to make amends is the key to Step Nine, and you can express that willingness in many different ways.

There are certain circumstances where making amends would cause more hurt than harmony. In those cases, you may be better off saying nothing and letting your changed behavior speak instead. Here again, you could still write an unsent letter of amends. It is always helpful to sort this out with someone like your sponsor who has experience with the Twelve Steps.

Is there someone on your Step Eight list to whom you cannot make amends? Write down what you would say to that person if you could make direct contact.

"We make amends to ourselves—to the personalities we were before becoming alcoholic—by understanding our sickness."
—*The Little Red Book*

Face Lingering Fears

Fear was a necessary reaction for primitive humans because it signaled real threats such as dangerous predators or bad weather. A healthy dose of fear makes you cautious and protective in an appropriate way, but the negative aspects of fear (anxiety, dread, worry, uncertainty, and apprehension) can paralyze you. Fear of the truth, for example, can fill you with dread and uncertainty and get in the way of your recovery.

A solid spiritual foundation helps you combat fear. When you feel afraid, meditate or pray. Listen to the guidance your Higher Power gives. You may also want to share your fears with your recovery group. If your fears are preventing you from living a full and balanced life, you may want to see a counselor or therapist to help you sort things out.

Read pages 63 and 75 in *Alcoholics Anonymous*. Write a prayer to your Higher Power about your fears, asking your Higher Power to calm your worries and help you to overcome your fears.

....

....

....

....

....

....

....

....

....

"Courage is fear that has said its prayers."

Give Back

Recovery requires you to reach out to others. Many—like Tom, a recovering alcoholic with twenty years of sobriety—discover that service helps them stay sober. "It's not just about helping other alcoholics; it's about learning to become a mirror in all areas of my life—to reflect back what I've learned from the program. And it's an opportunity to put my spirituality to work."

Helping others—leading a Twelve Step meeting, sharing your story, listening respectfully, giving of yourself without any expectation of reward or praise—is a way to practice humility. "You get to grow every time you help someone else. And you never know, maybe somewhere along the way, someone will see something in you that they need," said Tom.

Think about what Tom has to say about giving back and list some ways you can do the same. Describe how these actions help you practice humility.

....

....

....

....

....

....

....

....

....

"We become what we do."

Overcome Recovery Barriers

You overcome barriers to recovery when you work your program, attend meetings, pray, meditate, and strive to keep your life in balance. Practice conversation skills to become more at ease in social situations. Skip events where you suspect alcohol or other drugs are present. Acknowledge and deal with anger. Avoid loneliness by connecting with sober friends. Prevent fatigue by establishing a better sleep schedule. Stay centered by exercising and relaxing. Practice new ways of thinking through affirmations, and remember to give yourself credit for all the progress you've made.

Review your potential barriers to recovery and write down a solution or coping strategy for each. When your list is complete, make plans to learn new skills, develop new ways of thinking, and take concrete steps to keep your life in balance.

....

....

....

....

....

....

....

....

....

....

"If you don't want to slip, stay out of slippery places."

Practice Forgiveness

Forgiveness is a gift to yourself that frees you from the past. Renewing friendship is not always the goal, but letting go of hatred and rage should be. Once you decide to forgive, act "as if" you've already forgiven the person. Amazingly, your thinking usually changes once you've altered your behavior.

How would you act toward the person with whom you are in conflict if you didn't carry resentment? Would you be willing to extend an act of kindness? Would you let the conflict go and not perpetuate it?

Read page 66 in *Alcoholics Anonymous* about resentment. Picture the person toward whom you feel resentful. Now picture that person receiving a blessing in his or her life. When you no longer feel upset, angry, or jealous about this person's good fortune, then you are moving toward forgiveness. When you are capable of being truly happy for the person, then your forgiveness is complete.

Act as if you've already forgiven someone. Write down three actions of compassion and kindness you could take if you carried no resentment.

....

....

....

....

....

....

....

"Forgiveness is letting go of the idea that you could have had a different past."

Evaluate Your Progress

At this point in your recovery, you have already stretched yourself and grown as a result. You are beginning to incorporate the tools of Twelve Step recovery into your everyday life— sometimes without consciously knowing you are doing so. Describe times when you have noticed yourself accomplishing these recovery goals:

- surrendering to your Higher Power
- feeling humility instead of humiliation
- feeling spiritually fit
- being more of a student than a victim
- feeling that you are a part of something instead of separate
- feeling inspired
- learning from mistakes
- responding rather than reacting
- feeling happy, joyous, and free

....

....

....

....

....

....

....

"Change is inevitable, growth is intentional."
—Glenda Cloud

Let Go of Expectations

You can never be sure how someone will respond when you make amends for harm you have caused. You are responsible only for the effort, not the outcome. Some people will be supportive and impressed by your efforts, while others might be cautious or suspicious. Not everyone you approach to make amends will have a spiritual grounding, so you should not expect too much from each offended person. Even if the offended person stays offended, you will know that you've done your best. Overly optimistic expectations can set you up for disappointment. Making amends is about how *you* act, not how the other person reacts.

Read pages 76–84 in *Alcoholics Anonymous* about making amends. Are you working Step Nine as the Big Book suggests? Describe how it feels to begin the process of making amends.

....

....

....

....

....

....

....

....

....

....

"An expectation is a premeditated resentment."

Live with Gratitude

Gratitude reinforces the practice of taking a daily inventory because it is an antidote for many of your character defects. Self-centeredness, denial, isolation, living in the past, and other negative qualities dissolve because you check your ego at the door when you adopt an "attitude of gratitude."

You can learn to be more grateful with practice. Write down a list of only the positive gifts you are given each day. This practice silences your inner cynic and replaces negativity with positivity. When you practice Twelve Step gratitude, your glass is always at least half full. Do a gratitude inventory today.

....

....

....

....

....

....

....

....

....

....

"I am grateful that I found a recovery program that keeps me clean and sober and has led me to my Higher Power. Renewing that faith has changed my life. I've found a happiness and contentment I had forgotten existed. As long as I stay grateful, I'll stay clean and sober."

Be Authentic

Active addiction is like a Halloween party where you show up in disguise so people can't see who you really are. In recovery, you take off your mask and risk exposing the real you. This can be frightening at first, but the longer you go without your mask, the more you get used to showing your true face. And, miracle of miracles, people begin to accept you for who you really are—not the person you thought they wanted to see.

Describe someone in recovery whom you admire, someone who is authentic. What are some of that person's qualities? What does that person do to make you believe he or she is reflecting his or her true self? What do you do to practice your own authenticity?

....

....

....

....

....

....

....

....

....

....

"Pride is the mask of one's own faults."
—Jewish Proverb

Improve Important Relationships

Like all growth in recovery, growth in relationships is also a process. You have probably seen some positive changes in how you relate to others. Think about a couple of important relationships. Describe how you're practicing items from the following list:

- I ask my Higher Power for courage, and then I act as if I have courage.
- I am considerate of the needs of others.
- I ask for help when I need it.
- I am grateful and have learned to say thank you.
- I am willing to take action.
- I practice moderation, patience, tolerance, and forgiveness.
- I practice showing love and concern for others.
- I practice honesty and self-forgiveness.
- I am willing to trust my Higher Power and other people.

Review this list often to see how you are growing.

....

....

....

....

....

....

....

....

"The quality of our lives is dependent upon the quality of our relationships."

Grow Through Grief

Grief affects everyone at one time or another, but it is common in early recovery. Your addiction may have cost you relationships, marriage, custody of your children, social or economic status, health, or dreams. The stages of grief are often described as denial, anger, bargaining, depression, and acceptance.

It takes time to deal with grief, and you may need outside help, either from your recovery group or from a counselor. If you feel overwhelmed with grief, it is important to seek and accept support from others. Confide in your sponsor and recovery friends. Use Twelve Step meetings to share the grief you are experiencing.

If you are dealing with grief—even about something that happened more than a year ago—describe your feelings of loss. Try to be very detailed about how you felt about the loss and how you feel about it *now*. List a few people you can trust to help you understand and accept your feelings—and write down a date and time that you can talk with at least one of these people.

"You cannot prevent the birds of sorrow from flying overhead,
but you can prevent them from making nests in your hair."
—Chinese Proverb

Meditate on Positive Changes

Focus on the June 14 meditation from the book *Twenty-Four Hours a Day*: "It is not your circumstances that need altering so much as yourself. After you have changed, conditions will naturally change. Spare no effort to become all that God would have you become. Follow every good leading of your conscience. Take each day with no backward look. Face the day's problems with God, and seek God's help and guidance as to what you should do in every situation that may arise. Never look back. Never leave until tomorrow the thing that you are guided to do today."

Each day, think about what is going to motivate you to stay sober. Carry a medallion or key chain that reminds you of the importance of recovery to keep you motivated throughout the day. Describe something that helped keep you sober today.

....

....

....

....

....

....

....

....

....

....

"Sobriety is the gift that keeps on giving."

Heal Lingering Character Defects

Consider this story from a recovering addict: "I've used almost every substance there is: alcohol, cocaine, heroin, meth, and prescription medications. When I finally took a close look inside, I found that I suffered enormously from fear, self-pity, blaming, and anger, which fueled huge, ongoing resentments. I now realize that I used drugs to escape from these challenging feelings. In the old days, I would get drunk just to get back at someone. Performing a moral inventory forced me to identify, admit, and hand over these defects. When you really think about it, the concept is simple: If you let your character flaws go un-checked, eventually you will start drinking or using again. If you honestly admit your defects and hand them over to your Higher Power, you will clear a path back to your best self."

Read page 76 in *Alcoholics Anonymous.* Describe some of your lingering character defects and how they get in the way of your best self. Are you ready to admit these defects and hand them over to your Higher Power? If not, what is holding you back? What do you gain by holding on to character defects?

....

....

....

....

....

....

....

....

"I can't control what others do, but I can control my response."

Review Spiritual Principles

Each of the Twelve Steps contains a spiritual principle that is compatible with most religious traditions, whether you're Jewish, Christian, Muslim, Buddhist, agnostic, or something else:

1. Step One is about the *honesty* that emerges when you admit powerlessness.
2. Step Two is about the *hope* you acquire when you believe in a Higher Power.
3. Step Three is about the *faith* you gain when you "let go and let God."
4. Step Four is about the *courage* it takes to look within.
5. Step Five is about the *integrity* you achieve when you admit your wrongs.
6. Step Six is about the *willingness* to have your defects removed.
7. Step Seven is about embracing *humility*.
8. Step Eight is about gaining *compassion* to make amends.
9. Step Nine is about practicing *justice* by making amends.
10. Step Ten is about *perseverance* in continuing the journey.
11. Step Eleven is about the *spiritual awareness* you experience when you practice spirituality.
12. Step Twelve is about doing *service* as you share the Twelve Step message.

How are you doing with each of the Twelve Step principles that you have worked so far? Describe any problems or challenges, and discuss them with your sponsor at your next meeting.

....

....

....

....

....

"Principles before personalities."

Embrace Your True Self

Recovery is

- a developmental process of finding and building a new self
- a more grown-up way of being in the world
- not a move from bad to good, but from false to real
- growing emotionally and spiritually

Now that you've been in recovery for a while, you may wonder who you are without your addiction. In the past, your drug use became a substitute for what was missing inside your heart. It's important to honor this void and recognize that these feelings of longing are often healthy yearnings for spiritual growth—a tug at your sleeve that signals you are ready to transform, heal, and embrace your new spiritual self.

What things are most important to your heart? Think about the last time you really felt like the true you as a sober person. What was the experience like?

....

....

....

....

....

....

....

"I'm thankful for recovery because it gave me my identity. Before recovery I was whoever you needed me to be. Now I can be myself and that is okay."

Evaluate Your Recovery

On pages 83–84 in *Alcoholics Anonymous*, assurance is given that if you follow the advice in the Big Book and practice recovery each day, certain things—the "promises"—will come your way.

Evaluate your own recovery with the following "promises checklist." Rate each item based on the strength of your experience at this time. In what areas do you feel you are doing really well? In what areas are you still struggling? What changes could you make in those areas? Make a commitment to talk through the promises checklist with a recovery friend, and brainstorm ways you can continue to grow. Rate the following, from one to five (one is weak, five is strong):

____ amazement at your recovery progress
____ freedom and happiness
____ absence of regrets
____ serenity
____ benefit of experience with others
____ absence of self-pity
____ interest in others
____ absence of self-seeking behaviors
____ positive attitude
____ less fear of people and of economic insecurity
____ ability to handle difficulties
____ awareness of a Higher Power in your life

"Miracles take time."

Cultivate Positive Friendships

Some of your friends may not understand the disease of addiction and how important it is for you to stay away from situations that could cause cravings. If any of your current friendships lead you to put yourself in vulnerable situations, put your recovery first. Make a commitment to stay away from people and places that can cause you to return to drug use.

Cultivating sober friendships will help you avoid relapse. Twelve Step friends can support you because they understand your problems and can join you in sober, fun activities.

Write down one person in your support group with whom you could talk. Do you have that person's phone number? How could you start a conversation with him or her?

....

....

....

....

....

....

....

....

....

....

"Old friends pass, new friends appear. It is like days.
An old day passes, a new day arrives. The important thing
is to make it meaningful: a meaningful friend or a meaningful day."
—His Holiness the Dalai Lama

Replace Your Character Defects with Strengths

When your Higher Power removes your character defects, new strengths of character take their place, such as love, compassion, serenity, and gratitude.

Review your list of character defects, and for each one you've listed, write down a character strength to take its place in the form of an affirmation. Do this in the present tense, as if it has already occurred. For example, for "jealousy" you might write, "I am filled with trust." For pride you might write, "I am filled with humility and gratitude." After you have completed these affirmations, say them out loud. How does it feel to state them as a part of who you are?

....

....

....

....

....

....

....

....

....

....

....

"The qualities of a great person are vision, integrity, courage, understanding,
the power of articulation, and profundity of character."
—Adapted from a quote by Dwight Eisenhower

Keep Sharing Your Story

As you work the Steps and attend meetings, recovery becomes more about positive changes in your life than about your struggles and pain. You may discover you are becoming who you want to become. But you may also find that you still struggle with some issues.

One way to reflect on how far you've come is to tell your story to a newcomer at a meeting. Even if you have written it before, write out your story and plan a time to share it. Update it with more recent details and perspectives so you can see how far you've come. As you continue in recovery, your perspectives on your story may change.

Write down what you were like when you were using. What happened to get you into recovery? Who are you now, and how are you different than when you were actively using? Sharing your story not only helps you gain better perspective but also helps others.

....

....

....

....

....

....

....

....

"Fellowship is a big part of staying sober. We never go to a meeting
without taking something out of it, and we get more out of it
if we try to contribute something to it."

Keep Letting Go of Perfectionism

The Twelve Steps teach you to accept your limitations as an imperfect human being. Perfectionism can set you up for relapse because you may think your abstinence should be perfect. Challenge the self-defeating thoughts that fuel perfectionism by

- setting realistic and reachable goals. This will increase your sense of achievement and self-esteem.
- rethinking your idea of success. As long as you move forward, you are succeeding.
- enjoying the journey. Respect the energy, integrity, and time you dedicate to recovery and congratulate yourself for succeeding each day.
- recognizing that mistakes can be your greatest teachers.
- confronting your fears.

Give yourself a reality check by answering these questions:

- Have I set up impossible expectations for myself?
- What am I afraid of?
- What is the worst thing that could happen if I don't achieve my ultimate goal?

....

....

....

....

....

....

*"Many of us alcoholics use the excuse of not being able to
do something perfectly to enable us to do nothing at all . . .*
Have I stopped hiding behind the smokescreen of perfectionism?"
—*Twenty-Four Hours a Day,* November 23

Be Humble

You can achieve humility by serving, loving, and praying for others. When you practice humility, you understand your relationships better because you tolerate your own mistakes as well as those of others. You forgive, show respect, and act unselfishly. Instead of focusing on the flaws of others, you tend to your own life and issues.

You can practice humility by writing down the names of those you care about. Pray or meditate on their needs, and then write down ways you could help meet those needs.

....

....

....

....

....

....

....

....

....

....

*"If thou desire the love of God and man, be humble, for the proud heart,
as it loves none but itself, is beloved of none but itself. Humility enforces
where neither virtue, nor strength, nor reason can prevail."*
—Francis Quarles

Inventory Yourself as a Friend

Once a month, take an inventory of how you're doing as a friend. These questions can guide your inventory:

- Am I being honest with my friends in recovery?
- Am I being supportive and respectful of all my friends?
- Do I express love to my friends in both words and actions?
- Do I hold resentments toward any of my friends?
- Am I caring for my friends at the expense of my own needs?
- Am I humbly seeking wisdom and support from my friends?

Write down the answers to these questions, and note whether there are any particular friends with whom you're not being honest or supportive. That friendship may need a closer look.

....

....

....

....

....

....

....

....

"The only way to have a friend is to be one."
—Ralph Waldo Emerson

Review Your Relapse Response Plan

Things and people change, and your recovery strategies may have to be adjusted in order to accommodate life's changes. Even when your recovery is going well, you can't afford to let your guard down. Your relapse response plan is an important tool to help you. Consider asking your sponsor or a recovery friend to help you update your relapse response plan by answering the following questions:

- Do I need to update the high-risk people, places, things, and events to better reflect my current circumstances?
- Are certain times of day difficult for me?
- How do I handle my alone time?
- Am I facing any new high-risk habits, emotions, or situations?
- Do I need to update any positive or negative emotional states?
- Are there new social pressures that might endanger my recovery?
- Have I been in situations where I rationalize or deny?
- What changes do I need to make to achieve more balance?
- Should I update my relapse prevention contact list?

....

....

....

....

....

....

....

"An ounce of prevention is worth a pound of cure."

Congratulations for working on Step Nine! You are beginning to grow strong and true. If you notice your old ways and thoughts resurfacing, go back and review the lessons you learned in this Step.

Create Everyday Miracles

DAY 276 TO DAY 305

Take a Daily Inventory

Step Ten: "Continued to take personal inventory and when we were wrong promptly admitted it."

Step Ten involves an ongoing "spot check" of how you are doing each day in your recovery journey, whereas Step Four was the initial internal examination that allowed you to make peace with the past. Step Ten's daily self-examination is a sort of "balance sheet" where you acknowledge your successes (credits) as well as your mistakes (debits). With practice, noting your daily ups and downs will become second nature. If you are off course in any area, you can immediately address the relevant issues and avoid complacency and triggers that may threaten sobriety.

Read what page 84 in *Alcoholics Anonymous* says about the importance of Step Ten. Describe in your own words why you think it is important.

....

....

....

....

....

....

....

....

....

"By closing the day with a review of our emotional conduct
and our treatment of others, we can discover and correct
both our willfulness and mistakes."
—*The Little Red Book*

Look for Everyday Miracles

When you were drinking and using, you may have felt swallowed up in a world full of negativity. After spending almost a year in recovery, you may notice that you are more inclined to see the glass as half full, instead of half empty. Many people say that the spiritual change they have gone through has really opened their eyes to the everyday miracles that surrounded them all along.

Look around you. Are you beginning to notice when other people smile? Are you treasuring each day more fully? Do you laugh more easily? Are you more patient and tolerant than you were in your using days? List five things you observed today that made you smile or give thanks.

....

....

....

....

....

....

....

....

....

"Optimism: The doctrine or belief that everything is beautiful,
including what is ugly."
—Ambrose Bierce

Deepen Your Meditation

All religions have meditation disciplines, but meditation does not have to be religious. Meditation is the practice of focusing your attention on one thing—in a nonjudgmental way—in order to manage stress, get closer to your Higher Power, prevent or alleviate cravings, or manage symptoms such as pain. Meditation helps you see that you are not your thoughts or feelings, which come and go and are constantly changing. There are four elements basic to meditation:

- a quiet environment.
- an object to focus on, such as a candle flame, word, or prayer.
- a passive attitude so you can calm your thoughts and set aside your worries.
- a comfortable position. Most people sit, but you can also recline, kneel, stand, or walk.

You can meditate anywhere or anytime you have a quiet moment. Describe your experiences with meditation. If you haven't tried it yet, how do you think it could benefit you?

....

....

....

....

....

....

"We owe God both humility and respect; we show it
by freeing ourselves, for the moment, from material considerations . . .
and by giving Him our undivided attention."
—*The Little Red Book*

Develop an Attitude of Gratitude

Lasting recovery comes from trusting and staying connected with your Higher Power through prayer and meditation each day. *The Little Red Book* says that gratitude is the quality that sustains the miracle of sobriety: "As we develop gratitude we enlarge our capacity for happiness, service, and contented sobriety. A lack of gratitude may lead to that first drink; gratitude and sobriety go hand in hand." Some days, you may be thankful only for the fact that you are sober. On other days, you may have a whole list of blessings. When your heart is full of gratitude, there is little room for resentment.

Count your blessings. Cultivate an attitude of gratitude by listing what you are grateful for today.

....

....

....

....

....

....

....

....

....

....

"One single grateful thought raised to heaven is the most perfect prayer."
—G. E. Lessing

Start a Daily Personal Inventory

Step Ten strengthens recovery by helping you quickly resolve disagreements, face and admit wrongs, free yourself of guilt, and increase your joy.

Be aware of your thoughts, motives, words, and actions. Your Step Ten inventory will most likely turn up lots of difficult stuff from the past. You may discover you are still trying to prove yourself by acting superior to others. This is why recovery is called a journey rather than an event. Begin your Step Ten daily inventory by answering these questions:

- Have I used today?
- What can I be proud of today?
- How did I earn respect?
- How was I helpful?
- Have I practiced honesty, openness, and willingness?
- Have I prayed or meditated?
- Have I caused harm?
- Have I been my true self?
- Did I promptly ask my Higher Power to remove my defects?
- Did I promptly admit mistakes and make amends?
- Did I feel thankful?
- Did I feel sorry for myself?

"Step Ten makes us self-critical and less apt to criticize others.
It keeps us on the beam."
—*The Little Red Book*

Become Trustworthy

If you want to keep building genuine trust, keep working each day on being honest with yourself and others. It may be hard, but practice telling someone you trust about your feelings and thoughts. Talk about your goals and dreams, and listen to theirs. Being a good listener is an important component of trustworthiness.

How do you become more trustworthy? Keep taking responsibility. Practice being there for others. Ask important people in your life about how you can become more trustworthy. They might ask you to call when you're going to be late, or to always try to tell the complete truth.

Call some people you love today and ask how you might be more worthy of their trust. Ask your sponsor how trust was built in his or her relationships. List your discoveries here.

....

....

....

....

....

....

....

....

....

....

"We learn to trust by becoming trustworthy."

Make It a Good Day

Your daily inventory will challenge you. You may discover that you are still trying to prove yourself as "good enough" to others. You may confront something that will cause you pain and grief, such as rejection, guilt, shame, anger, or a defeat that you haven't let go of.

If you make mistakes or are off course in any area of your life, the sooner you admit it, the better chance you have of getting back on the right track. Don't beat yourself up about past mistakes. And don't hold resentments against others for things that happened in the past. Each person is a work in progress. Each person is good enough in the eyes of a Higher Power. No matter what has happened in the past, you are worthy. You've already made amends; now take on the world one day at a time. You are responsible for what you do today. Make it a good day.

Do you feel good enough or are you still trying to prove yourself to others? What things are you holding on to from the past that cause you pain or insecurity? Do you need to feel like you're better than others? Would making more money or achieving more make you different than you are right now? Talk with your sponsor about things from the past that hold you back.

....

....

....

....

....

....

....

....

"Things do not change; we change."
—Henry David Thoreau

Tune In to Your Higher Power

As you work the Steps, you've been repairing the damage of your past and creating a new, healthier way to live. You've had to trust your Higher Power as a reliable guide. It's not always easy to maintain this type of faith and perseverance. The messages and guidance from your Higher Power can be difficult to understand. Your desires, emotions, and opinions are so ingrained that sometimes the will of your Higher Power is distorted by your own feelings and wants. What you want in your life today may not be what you need. Trust in your Higher Power to be a wiser guide than you can be. Look at the progress you have made so far, keep letting go of your self-will, and trust that there is a greater force at work that wants the best for you.

Meditate today to tune in to your Higher Power. What things are you trying to create in your life that may not be what you need? Can you let go of these things? Share your feelings with a close friend in recovery. You may find that your friend has been through the very same thoughts and feelings.

....

....

....

....

....

....

....

....

"I can experience many miracles today if I am willing to change my mind."

Deal with Emotions One Day at a Time

It's sometimes difficult for people in recovery to know what normal is. You may wonder whether everyone feels the things you feel or whether it's okay to feel what you're feeling. You might be afraid to be happy or feel good because it might signal to you that you're being selfish or not taking care of others. You may worry that if you feel good today, you'll pay for it tomorrow because something bad is sure to happen.

This uncertainty is a common struggle for people in recovery—and for people in general. The key is to be patient, acknowledge whatever you feel, and continue to find healthy ways to express those feelings. Rest assured that others have had the same feelings you have, and know that emotions do not last forever. The fact that you feel them at all is another sign that you are growing in recovery.

Do you avoid certain challenging feelings? Describe these fears, and then discuss them with your sponsor or a recovery friend to learn coping skills.

....

....

....

....

....

....

....

....

"Thoughts are not things and feelings are not facts;
they only have the power we give them."

Keep It Real

Research has shown that people who relapse often focus on the immediate positive benefits of using drugs. When exposed to conflict or stress, you may start to think about how using will help you deal with pain, anger, or inadequacy. Instead, remember how far you have come in recovery and how spiritually powerful your life has become. Think about the negative consequences of drinking or using. You could lose your family, friends, career, or children. Don't let the idea of instant gratification cause you to compromise all the things you want for your life. If you start to think about how good using would feel, call your sponsor immediately.

Describe the negative consequences of drug use in your life. Remind yourself daily that use isn't worth it.

"While we may not be able to control all that happens to us,
we can control what happens inside us."
—Benjamin Franklin

Keep Asking for Help

Now that you're well into your first year of recovery, you may feel pretty confident about your ability to stay clean and sober. Overconfidence can put your sobriety in jeopardy because the moment you let your guard down, you make yourself vulnerable to relapse. Even though you've made lots of progress, you still need to work every day to keep your disease—addiction—in remission. Always keep your support list handy, and make sure there is someone you trust whom you can call for help at any time.

Review your list of support people to see whether it has changed. Talk to the first and second people on the list regularly to keep the lines of communication open. Practice checking in with your sponsor when you know that you will face a stressful situation, such as going to a work party or handling a relationship issue. Give back by listening to your support person and being invested in his or her health and spiritual growth as well.

Call a support person today and describe how the check-in went. Was there a balanced give-and-take?

....

....

....

....

....

....

....

....

"He who is afraid of asking for help is afraid of learning."

Accept What Happens Today

Acceptance is coming to terms with what is: the good, the bad, and the confusing things life hands us every day. When you learn acceptance, you become more honest with yourself and others. You start letting go of judgments that block you from seeing things as they really are. Each day holds joys and challenges. You might get a promotion at work one day, and your car may break down the next. Accepting these realities without denying or resisting will allow you to see life as a rich fabric woven of many and varied experiences.

List three realities of today and precede them with the phrase "I accept." Can you feel the inner shift that occurs when you accept what is happening right now?

....

....

....

....

....

....

....

....

....

....

....

"Life is 10 percent what you make it and 90 percent how you take it."

Reduce Complacency

The Little Red Book describes Step Ten as the "slide rule for quick mental reckoning" of daily progress in recovery. This daily check-in is a way to stay on course and remind yourself that no matter how confident and good you may be feeling, you are—and always will be—a person in recovery from a life-threatening disease.

Complacency in recovery is a false sense of contentment that can lower your guard and let defects like intolerance and resentment creep back in. If you aren't careful, you can find yourself getting a little lax about honesty, humility, or making amends.

How are you doing with your daily inventory? What things can you do to avoid complacency this week?

"Don't let your special character and values get swallowed up
by the great chewing complacency."
—Aesop

Heal from Emotional Pain

Consider this story from a forty-year-old recovering methamphetamine addict with nine months of sobriety: "Before I got into treatment, I almost lost my wife and my children. They went to live with relatives, and I didn't know whether they would come back. The fear of that loss got me to make a commitment to abstain from using and to concentrate on my recovery. It was scary to face the world for the first time without being high to numb my pain. Going to meetings and talking with others who had suffered similar losses made me aware that grief can remind us of our great capacity to love and to heal."

Reflect on your own experiences of grief. Are there things that have happened in your life that are still causing you emotional pain? Describe what happened and how you feel about it. Make sure you call one person, preferably your sponsor or another person in recovery, to talk about these feelings of pain and loss.

....

....

....

....

....

....

....

....

"[God's] spirit shall flow through me and, in flowing through me, it shall sweep away all the bitter past. I will take heart. The way will open for me."
—*Twenty-Four Hours a Day,* January 3

Rebuild Trust with Friends and Family

Of your best friends and family, who supports your recovery and overall health? These are the relationships you need to cultivate. These relationships may have been damaged in the past by things you did while you were using. One way to rebuild trust is to accept your supportive friends and family exactly as they are, rather than trying to change or control them. Focus on the positive traits they bring to the relationship.

Try to think about the other person's needs, while staying aware of your own. Ask what you can do to be a better friend and follow through on what they ask for. Ask your Higher Power to help you build relationships and grow in them.

Think about your most supportive friends or family, and ask yourself what you can do to rebuild their trust in you.

....

....

....

....

....

....

....

....

....

....

"TEAM = Together Everyone Achieves More"

Keep Celebrating the Benefits of Recovery

Recovery is truly the gift that keeps on giving. You have probably already gained some benefits in your improved relationships with friends, family, and co-workers. You may have experienced more moments of peace and serenity and developed a stronger connection to your Higher Power. You may have noticed that you have more patience and a better ability to deal with problems.

List fifteen other benefits you feel you have gained from being in recovery. Make a copy of this list and carry it with you. Focusing on the benefits of recovery can be a great motivator to keep you on track during difficult times.

....

....

....

....

....

....

....

....

....

....

"GIFT = God Is Forever There"

Deal with Problems in Making Amends

Pages 66–67 in *Alcoholics Anonymous* talk about letting go of anger and unmet expectations. When you make amends to someone, you might think, "Okay, I've owned up and taken responsibility for my actions in our falling out. Now I'm ready for your apology." But the apology you expect may not come, and you might find yourself growing angry over the injustice of the situation.

The Big Book urges you to look at others with compassion, recognizing that they might also suffer from the spiritual malady that plagued you before you began your journey of recovery. It reminds you to take your own inventory instead of concentrating on the faults or fears of others. The important thing is to practice humility, asking your Higher Power for tolerance and patience for yourself and guidance for your friend.

Write a prayer of compassion for someone with whom you have been in conflict. How does it feel to humbly accept responsibility for your actions while letting go of expectations that others will do the same?

"An eye for an eye would make the whole world blind."
—Mohandas Gandhi

Continue to Embrace the True You

A major task in recovery is to define who you are, not just as an alcoholic or addict, but also as a lovable, capable person worthy of respect and love from others. You nurture and reconnect with the "true you" when you focus on your positive traits—those special qualities that make you the unique person you are.

Take a moment and list adjectives that describe you, such as loyal, honest, trustworthy, hopeful, or shy. Don't just list your roles, such as parent, employee, or student. Go deeper. Scratch beneath the surface of yourself to uncover, then embrace, the true you.

....

....

....

....

....

....

....

....

....

....

....

"Knowing others is wisdom; knowing the self is enlightenment."
—Lao-tzu

Watch Out for Resentment

Resentment is unresolved anger you keep alive by replaying a scene or conversation in your mind and dredging up the hurt again and again. You are the one who suffers when you hold on to resentments because these feelings feed on themselves and can threaten your recovery. Pages 63–65 in *Alcoholics Anonymous* tell how to inventory resentments.

As you perform your everyday inventory to investigate how you feel and react to daily life, remember to identify and describe any lingering or growing resentments. To do so, answer these questions:

- What is the cause of the resentment? (What happened? Why are you angry?)
- How does the cause of your resentment affect you? (Does it affect your self-esteem, pride, emotional or financial security, ambitions, or relationships?)
- What part did you play? (Were you dishonest, selfish, fearful, or inconsiderate?)

What behavior patterns do you recognize, and which need the most work? How can you prevent future resentments?

....

....

....

....

....

....

....

"It does not pay to nurse a grudge, it hurts us more than anyone else . . .
If we are resentful, we will be resented."
—*Twenty-Four Hours a Day,* November 7

Promptly Admit When You Are Wrong

Taking a daily inventory is just the first part of Step Ten. The second part is admitting your wrongs. It's important to do this right away, before more damage is done. You may want to enlist the help of your sponsor or a recovery friend so you can get their feedback on how well you're doing. This is a great exercise in humility. It is a reminder that you are not always the most objective person when it comes to taking your own inventory.

Plan a regular time to take a personal inventory with a supportive person. After doing your inventory, consider doing a role-play with him or her to practice the process of admitting you are wrong. Describe how you feel about doing a daily inventory, and who might help you with it.

....

....

....

....

....

....

....

....

"We make the inventory a sort of intelligence department
that identifies old and new moral defects . . . So when self-centeredness,
for instance, disguises itself as complacency or boredom,
we detect the deception, then arrest and treat it."
—*The Little Red Book*

Continue to Take a Daily Inventory

As you are discovering, recovery is an ongoing and lifelong process that you engage in each and every day. It is important to monitor how you're doing each day so you don't lose ground or slip back into your old unhealthy habits. Review pages 84–85 in *Alcoholics Anonymous* about the importance of a daily inventory. Then find a quiet time and place to reflect on your day.

Write down what has gone well and what has not. Ask your Higher Power to remove obstacles, such as complacency, fear, or pride, that inhibit you from honest self-reflection. Remember to take your own inventory—not someone else's—and jot down the areas you need to work on.

....

....

....

....

....

....

....

....

....

*"[Step Ten's] purpose is to remind us that moral defects—selfishness,
dishonesty, resentment, and fear—are still problems we will encounter daily."*
—The Little Red Book

Enjoy the Benefits of Working Step Ten

Performing a daily inventory is like taking your temperature to make certain a dormant illness hasn't re-emerged—in your case, the disease is addiction. You've learned how your chemical dependency affects so many others, so it makes good sense to monitor your disease each day and reduce the risk of possible contagion.

Pages 84–85 in *Alcoholics Anonymous* tell addicts what they can expect as a result of working Step Ten:

- You will no longer have unresolved conflict with anyone or anything—even alcohol or other drugs.
- You will recover your sanity.
- You will be less interested in alcohol and drugs.
- You will be more aware of temptations.
- You will naturally react more sanely to challenges.
- You will no longer have to focus on fighting the urge to use.
- You will feel safe and protected.
- You will become spiritually fit and content with being who you are.

Review this list. Describe any benefits you've experienced from doing a daily inventory.

....

....

....

....

....

....

"We are not cured of addiction. What we really have is a daily reprieve,
contingent on the maintenance of our spiritual condition."
—Adapted from *Twenty-Four Hours a Day*, August 28

Start Your Day with Prayer and Meditation

Page 86 in *Alcoholics Anonymous* suggests that you start your day with a morning prayer in order to prepare your heart and mind for the day ahead. Prayer and meditation remind you that you're not in charge. When you ask your Higher Power for daily guidance, your will and self-absorption lessen, and you are better able to focus on those around you. Start out by allowing five to ten minutes for this time of prayer and meditation.

As you practice, you may find that this contemplative time increases, or you might discover you enjoy taking a few minutes throughout the day and evening to slow down and meditate. Breathe deeply to slow your mind, or read a poem or passage from a meditation book to get settled.

What are some benefits of making prayer and meditation a central part of your life?

....

....

....

....

....

....

....

....

....

....

"Help me set aside what I think I know, so I can be teachable today."

Get Creative with Meditation

There is no right or wrong way to meditate or pray, and no perfect place in which to do it. If you pay attention and expand your ideas of what contemplative time means, you'll discover there are many opportunities all around you each day. You might

- say the Serenity Prayer (see Day 17) during breaks throughout the day
- start your meditation time with inspirational music
- spend time in quiet reflection during a traffic jam
- listen to audio meditation books when you're in the car
- consider attending retreats or programs for spiritual growth
- use hobbies, such as gardening or fishing, as opportunities to meditate or pray
- make a conscious effort to slow down and be quiet by turning off the television and radio

Try some of the suggestions above, and then describe your experience.

....

....

....

....

....

....

....

....

"Act as if what you do makes a difference. It does."
—William James

Keep Working Your Recovery Program

Consider this story from a cocaine addict with two years of sobriety: "Even though I've been abstinent for two years, I still need my sponsor, family, other group members, and clean-and-sober friends in order to really protect my recovery. My friends and family understand that it's a lifelong process, and they are committed to helping me keep working hard, year after year. I make my recovery a priority by continuing to examine the goals and values I set for my life, and I make improvements where I can. This is one of my favorite parts of recovery. I look forward to all the positive changes I can make in the future."

Reflect on this story. Is your recovery still your top priority? Do you look at your recovery work every day and make improvements where you can? Describe one positive change you can make this week to make your recovery a bigger priority—whether giving back to others at meetings or saying a quick morning prayer or meditation to focus your day on what is important to you. Look forward to this opportunity for change. No matter how well you are doing, there is always room for growth.

....

....

....

....

....

....

....

....

"By failing to prepare, you are preparing to fail."
—Benjamin Franklin

Give Back at Meetings

As you grow more comfortable in your recovery, you will become more aware and appreciative of the gifts of wisdom, support, and understanding that are given to you at meetings. Recovering people often say, "In order to keep it, you have to give it away." In time, you will understand the deep value of sharing your energy, time, and experience with others in meetings. You will be ready to welcome a frightened newcomer or stay late to talk with someone who is struggling. You might go to a meeting reluctantly, thinking you don't need it, only to discover that the meeting needed you.

Practice giving back at a meeting this week by showing up early, welcoming a newcomer, sharing your story, or staying late to listen to a person in need. Describe the experience. How did your perspective on meetings change?

....

....

....

....

....

....

....

....

....

....

"In order to keep it, you have to give it away."

Keep Practicing Spirituality

The Big Book says that every day is an opportunity to carry your Higher Power's will into your life. But practicing daily spirituality requires diligence and intentionality. Ask your Higher Power to keep you company as you examine your day. If you like, take a deep breath or take a moment to do a meditation exercise to settle in.

Walk through your day, event by event, first looking for the blessings you were given. Then pick an event that brought up negative feelings and acknowledge any wrongs you did. Close with a prayer or use the Step Ten prayer on page 85 in *Alcoholics Anonymous*.

Did this meditative practice connect you more closely with your Higher Power? Can you maintain an intentional attitude tomorrow as you walk with your Higher Power throughout the day?

....

....

....

....

....

....

....

....

....

....

"My life became so much richer when I learned to live in the mystery,
in conscious contact with my Higher Power."

Monitor Your Emotions

Now that you've had some time in recovery, you may find that many of your emotions have settled down, and it is easier to manage them. However, it is common to still feel things like loneliness, grief, a need for high drama, or anger and resentment from time to time.

Remember that feelings are neither good nor bad; they are what they are. But they are *not* facts. When uncomfortable emotions arise, express them in a calm and healthy way. Count to ten before responding, or leave the situation until you feel able to discuss it. Talk with your sponsor about what is bothering you, and ask for ideas on how to resolve things. You may choose just to let something go, realizing that the situation is out of your control and it's best just to accept it.

Review Step Ten and list some of the emotions that keep creeping up in your daily inventory. Make a commitment to talk to your sponsor about feelings that interfere with your recovery.

....

....

....

....

....

....

....

....

....

"Feel it, deal with it, and then heal from it."

Live Happy, Joyous, and Free

Even those with many months of sobriety can exhibit "dry drunk" traits: a return to addictive thinking and behavior without actually using drugs or alcohol. You might say that "dry drunk" happens when you take the rum out of the fruitcake, but you still have the fruitcake! Are you often

- unrealistic about your own abilities?
- highly critical of others?
- intolerant of another's mistakes or differences?
- unable to make up your mind?
- prone to acting without thinking?
- dishonest?
- used to pressuring others to get what you want?
- inconsiderate?

Living sober is more than just stopping alcohol and other drug use. It's about living happy, joyous, and free as you remain abstinent. If you answered yes to any of the above questions, you may be living in a state of "dry drunk." Talk to your sponsor, and then list what you can do to change your attitude so you can begin living happy, joyous, and free.

....

....

....

....

....

....

"Success is not the key to happiness. Happiness is the key to success."
—Albert Schweitzer

Expect the Unexpected

Are you someone who is in the habit of checking the weather forecast on your computer or television before you head out to a picnic, athletic event, or vacation? Have you ever planned an outdoor party and worried whether it would rain or even snow unexpectedly?

Staying vigilant in recovery is like checking the weather. You never know when your sobriety will be put to the test. You could run into an old using buddy or find yourself in a sudden emotional crisis that threatens your recovery.

Even though you may feel confident about your sobriety and your life right now, be prepared for unexpected situations or personal encounters that cause you to risk relapse. Envision recovery as the jacket you keep handy in case there's a change in the weather. Go to meetings. Check in with your sponsor. Keep working the Steps. Always be prepared to protect your recovery.

List the strategies you have in place if unexpected things arise that threaten your recovery.

....

....

....

....

....

....

....

....

"You better live your best and act your best and think your best today, for today is the sure preparation for tomorrow and all the other tomorrows that follow."
—Harriet Martineau

Congratulations for working on Step Ten! You are begin-ning to create everyday miracles. If you notice your old ways and thoughts resurfacing, go back and review the lessons you learned in this Step.

Find Peace in Spirituality

DAY 306 TO DAY 335

Listen to Your Higher Power

Step Eleven: "Sought through prayer and meditation to improve our conscious contact with God *as we understood Him,* praying only for knowledge of His will for us and the power to carry that out."

You've begun to create a healthier way to live, unburdened by the past and more appreciative of the present. Along the way, you've learned to trust your Higher Power as a dependable guide who helps you discover and maintain serenity. Step Eleven asks you to continue to pray and meditate in order to improve your relationship with your Higher Power. When you pray, you converse with your Higher Power; when you meditate, you listen. If you need concrete evidence that this process works, just look at the miracles that have happened so far. Continue to trust the process, "praying only for knowledge" of your Higher Power's will and the power to carry that will out.

Take some quiet time to write an Eleventh Step prayer thanking your Higher Power and asking for continued guidance. Then meditate and listen for what your Higher Power has to say.

....

....

....

....

....

....

....

"Planning our day, we ask for knowledge of God's will
and for divine direction that we may make right decisions.
Our prayers should be unselfish and useful to others."
—*The Little Red Book*

Let Go of the Need to Be Perfect

Perfectionism is not about excellence; it's about unrealistic standards. If you beat yourself up and feel like a failure for making mistakes instead of seeing mistakes as a natural part of your growth, you may have perfectionist tendencies. Demanding perfection of yourself leads to frustration and low self-esteem, and it threatens your recovery. If your expectations of others are unreasonably high, your perfectionism is probably causing stress, judgment, and disappointment while limiting your relationships with others. Alcoholics Anonymous cofounder Bill W. said that alcoholics often try to overcome their human limitations by playing God. Remember, you can't will yourself to be perfect, just as you can't will yourself sober. Redefine your idea of personal success by giving yourself permission to make mistakes.

Embrace the fact that you are human and that mistakes are a natural part of growth. Describe three recent mistakes you made and what you learned from each.

....

....

....

....

....

....

....

....

"I have not failed. I've just found 10,000 ways that won't work."
—Thomas Edison

Keep Asking for Help

There's a reason Twelve Step groups refer to members as "recovering" instead of "recovered"—no matter how many months or years they've been sober. You're working on spiritual *progress,* not perfection. And recovery is a lifelong process.

You may have grown comfortable in your recovery and gotten used to helping out at meetings—welcoming newcomers, setting up chairs, making coffee, or sharing your story. You may even be helping someone else in recovery as a sponsor or support person. But when did you last seek help?

Chances are good that you still have times of confusion, days of challenge, and problems that arise in your family, work, or social life. Asking your sponsor or a trusted friend to lend an ear is an exercise in humility and a way to keep your recovery strong and on track. Asking for help with things like car problems or home improvement projects is another way to maintain an "attitude of gratitude."

Do you ask for help? Describe how it feels to continue to reach out.

....

....

....

....

....

....

....

....

....

"HELP = Hope, Encouragement, Love, Patience"

Trust Yourself by Trusting Others

As you progress in your recovery and find deeper spiritual connections, you'll find that others are starting to trust you more. But you also build trust by trusting and sharing with others. When people in your meeting are open and honest with you, it is easier to be open and honest with them. When you see others being reliable and compassionate, it feels safer to rely on them, and you learn that you can also be reliable and compassionate.

List some ways others are starting to trust you more now that you are in recovery. How do you see this in your daily life?

....

....

....

....

....

....

....

....

....

....

"Few things help an individual more than to place responsibility upon him,
and to let him know that you trust him."
—Booker T. Washington

Deepen Your Spirituality

Spirituality is the quality of your relationship with yourself, your Higher Power, close friends and family, and the world. It includes your values, your priorities, the way you interact with others, and your concept of a Higher Power. Start improving your spiritual connections with these steps:

- Take time to pray (talk to your Higher Power).
- Take time to meditate (listen to your Higher Power).
- Connect with and appreciate other people every day.
- Appreciate the positive changes you see within yourself.

Describe a few things you will do this week to improve your spiritual connections. What spiritual changes have you experienced since you started recovery?

....

....

....

....

....

....

....

....

"Saying thank you is more than good manners. It is good spirituality."
—Alfred Painter

Recover from Lost Relationships

Addiction hurts intimate relationships, sometimes beyond repair. You may want to consider marital counseling if you are having problems relating to or reconnecting with your spouse or partner. If divorce, separation, or a breakup seems to be the only option, increase contact with your support network and attend more meetings. Focus on recovery and work the Steps. Grieve, but don't obsess about the past because that can lead to blaming, resentment, and anger—all of which threaten your sobriety. Avoid isolation, stay away from relapse triggers, and celebrate the good things in life with sober friends. If children are involved, put them first and reassure them that the breakup isn't their fault. Let them know you will be actively involved in their lives no matter what happens.

Describe any problems you are experiencing in an intimate relationship. How are these problems affecting your recovery? Call your sponsor or another sober person for support.

....

....

....

....

....

....

....

....

....

"The past is beyond recall. The future is as uncertain as life itself.
Only the now belongs to us. Am I living in the now?"
—*Twenty-Four Hours a Day,* June 30

Get Centered

Find a quiet spot where you can rest without distraction. Repeat this meditation: "Breathe in the inspiration of goodness and truth. It is the spirit of honesty, purity, unselfishness, and love. It is readily available if I am willing to accept it wholeheartedly. God has given me two things—his spirit and the power of choice—to accept or not, as I will. I have the gift of free will. When I choose the path of selfishness and greed and pride, I am refusing to accept God's spirit. When I choose the path of love and service, I accept God's spirit and it flows into me and makes all things new."

Reflect on ways you have been honest and unselfish this week. Describe how you felt. Think about ways you can use your free will for love and goodness. If you were selfish or greedy, make note of those behaviors. During the next twenty-four hours, practice spirituality by being loving toward and patient with all God's creatures—even those that frustrate or challenge you.

"The future belongs to those who believe in the beauty of their dreams."
—Eleanor Roosevelt

Continue to Make Amends

A person in recovery likened hurting someone to punching a hole in the street. The longer the hole is left untended, the more that wear and water will make it bigger and bigger, until the hole grows so large it swallows up anything that drives into it. Making amends is a way to repair the hole your actions have caused. Amends smooth the road to recovery, regardless of the other person's actions or reactions. It is an ongoing process that helps you maintain an attitude of humility and develop a heightened sense of compassion for the feelings of others.

Are you continuing to make amends when you do or say something that harms others? Has the process of making amends gotten easier for you as you grow stronger in your recovery?

"Have I taken an inventory of myself and admitted the wrong I have done? Have I come clean with my friends? Have I tried to make it up to them for the way I have treated them?"
—*Twenty-Four Hours a Day,* January 4

Continue to Grow in Spirituality

As you continue to grow in recovery, you continue to grow spiritually. By making prayer and meditation a central part of your life, you

- focus on your Higher Power's will
- are better prepared for whatever arises during the day
- can better process whatever happens
- can pray for others, which helps you let go of anger and resentment
- can remember that you are a recovering addict

There is no right way or amount of time to pray or meditate. Some people focus on breathing to slow their minds; others like to read a meditation. Do what feels best for you. As you practice prayer and meditation, you get better at accepting that not every opportunity in life is your Higher Power's will for you.

Write down and complete the following prayer, and make a commitment to say it every day: "Help me set aside what I think I know about _____, so I can be teachable today."

....

....

....

....

....

....

....

"I pray that I may accept my Higher Power's direction in my life's journey."
—Adapted from *Twenty-Four Hours a Day,* July 5

Keep Celebrating Growth

Awhile back, you listed some of the benefits you have gained from being in recovery. It is important to realize what a divine gift your recovery is to others too. What improvements have you seen in your relationships? How have your interpersonal connections changed or grown as a result of your being in recovery? Although you are in recovery for yourself, this program is a gift for those who support and love you.

Reflect on your recovery so far. List some of the positive ways in which it has affected others. What changes have you observed as a result of your spiritual growth?

....

....

....

....

....

....

....

....

....

....

....

"We are happy when we are growing."
—William Butler Yeats

See the Good

Find a quiet spot where you can rest without distraction. Read the September 3 meditation from the book *Twenty-Four Hours a Day*: "The spiritual life depends upon the Unseen. To live the spiritual life, you must believe in the Unseen. Try not to lose the consciousness of God's spirit in you and in others. As a child in its mother's arms, stay sheltered in the understanding and love of God. God will relieve you of the weight of worry and care, misery and depression, want and woe, faintness and heartache, if you will let Him. Lift up your eyes from earth's troubles and view the glory of the unseen God. Each day try to see more good in people, more of the Unseen in the seen."

Describe some things that are worrying you this week. Take those things and hand them to your Higher Power for today.

....

....

....

....

....

....

....

....

....

"Each time you see the good in another person, you are being spiritual."

Develop Deeper Spirituality

In the first year of recovery, it's important to abstain from drinking and identify high-risk situations. *But the foundation of your ongoing recovery is spiritual.*

When you were using substances, you likely "played God," acting as if you had ultimate control over your life. You were "right," and others needed to conform to your way of seeing things. You searched for happiness but found a spiritual void. You tried to fill that void with alcohol or other drugs, which never worked for long. If you stop growing spiritually, you'll likely return to active addiction.

Think about ways you "played God" while you were using. Did you think your way was the right way? Did you expect others to do things your way? Write about ways of thinking that got in the way of your spirituality.

....

....

....

....

....

....

....

....

....

....

"The Twelve Steps work whether or not you believe in God,
but they won't work very well if you believe you are God."

Watch Out for Self-Defeating Behaviors

Ninety-eight percent of what you do in life is by habit, and sometimes those habits can impede your progress in recovery. What you live with you learn, what you learn you practice, what you practice you become, and what you become has consequences.

Although habitual behaviors can be a problem, habitual thinking can also get you into trouble. Have you gotten into the habit of thinking any of the following?

- My life should be pain-free.
- Everything should always go my way.
- I should always be in control.
- Life should always be fair.
- I shouldn't need to ask for help.

What persistent thoughts are getting in the way of your recovery? What can you do to let go of them?

....

....

....

....

....

....

....

"The chains of habit are generally too small to be felt until they are too strong to be broken."
—Samuel Johnson

Stay Grounded

Consider this story from a recovering addict: "After I had been sober for a year, I wanted to test my willpower by going with friends to bars and parties. I even started to think that I could drink just one beer and stop there. I could tell that my self-will was longing to run riot again. I talked to my sponsor, and he helped me focus my new confidence on helping others instead of focusing on myself. I began to speak at meetings and stay late to counsel others. This keeps me grounded and helps me remember that I'm not the center of the universe. As I watch other people get better, I learn how to improve my own recovery. When they stumble, they show me what mistakes to avoid."

Over time, self-will can creep back into your life and block you from your Higher Power. That's why going to meetings and talking with others in recovery will keep you grounded.

Describe some ways self-will or arrogance gets in your way. Make a commitment to surrender to a lifestyle of love, gratitude, and humility.

....

....

....

....

....

....

....

....

"When I started to change, I began a never-ending spiritual journey.
I no longer battled against my life. I learned to love my life."

Renew Healthy Relationships

Addiction has a profound effect on relationships, causing significant damage. In the past, your substance abuse competed with your relationships, and in all likelihood, your substance abuse won the battle. Growth in relationships is a process, like growth in recovery, and you've probably already experienced some positive changes in how you relate to others.

Spend a few minutes reflecting on the status of some of your more important relationships. Write down the way you act in them, and ask yourself what is working well and what is not working. Make a commitment to tell others how much you appreciate them.

....

....

....

....

....

....

....

....

....

"Friends are now people who understand me and I them,
whom I can help and who can help me to live a better life.
I have learned not to hold back and wait for friends to come to me,
but to go halfway and to be met halfway, openly and freely."
—*Twenty-Four Hours a Day,* October 30

Learn from Mistakes

Everyone makes mistakes. It's natural that you will experience a few slip-ups in the first year of recovery. For example, you may have attended a work party where you knew alcohol would be served. To make the situation worse, you might have forgotten to bring your contact list of support people that you could call for help. You may have made amends to someone, and then undone the progress by saying something offensive out of anger or hurt. You may have even taken a drink or gone back to your old stash to see what you could find to use. Don't let any of these things get you down. If you make a mistake, talk with your sponsor immediately. He or she will help you take responsibility for what happened—and get you back on track.

If you return to use, it's especially important to stop using and call your sponsor immediately. No one is perfect. But you can strive to learn from your mistakes rather than beat yourself up.

Describe some mistakes you have made recently. Take responsibility for your part in the situation. Describe what you could have done differently to cause a better outcome.

....

....

....

....

....

....

....

*"Each day will unfold something good, as long as I am trying to live
the way I believe God wants me to live."*
—*Twenty-Four Hours a Day,* January 3

Handle Work Challenges

Recovery isn't about eliminating challenges and stress from your life; it is about developing strategies to cope with difficulties when they do arise. There will be times when you encounter slippery situations at work that could lead to relapse if you are not prepared ahead of time. You may have to travel out of town on business or celebrate a promotion of a co-worker. Maybe you'll be asked to attend a holiday party where alcohol will flow freely.

Think about possible work situations that could threaten your sobriety, and list safe ways to handle them. How could you find a local Twelve Step meeting if you are out of town? Whom could you call if your sponsor is not available? If you don't know the answers to these questions, ask your sponsor for help.

"To be prepared is half the victory."
—Miguel de Cervantes

Discover the Realm of the Spirit

Find a quiet moment to read the April 19 meditation from the book *Twenty-Four Hours a Day*: "It is a glorious way—the upward way. There are wonderful discoveries in the realm of the spirit. There are tender intimacies in the quiet times of communion with God. There is an amazing, almost incomprehensible understanding of the other person. On the upward way, you can have all the strength you need from that Higher Power. You cannot make too many demands on Him for strength. He gives you all the power you need, as long as you are moving along the upward way."

Describe times when you have looked "upward" this week and connected with your Higher Power. How did this connection affect your daily life?

....

....

....

....

....

....

....

....

....

....

"I can experience many miracles today if I'm willing to change my mind."

Find New Ways to Give Back

The Twelve Step program emphasizes how thoughts and actions shape lives. Words and acts of kindness, generosity, thoughtfulness, and forgiveness make us more kind, generous, thoughtful, and forgiving. The Big Book stresses that a spiritual life is not just a theory; you have to live it.

When you feel ready, consider being a support person for someone else. Be available to talk with others in recovery. Speak to others about the disease of addiction. Keep telling your own recovery story, which becomes more powerful the longer you stay in recovery. Be an example and an advocate for people who struggle—as you struggle—to stay sober.

Approach someone at a meeting this week whom you sense needs support. Describe how it felt to do this. How do you think such acts strengthen your own recovery? List some other ways you can give back.

"If you want others to be happy, practice compassion.
If you want to be happy, practice compassion."
—His Holiness the Dalai Lama

Keep Thinking Positively

You can't control anyone else's actions, but you can control your own reactions. There is usually something positive—a lesson to be learned, an insight to be gained—even in the bleakest of moments.

Describe a recent event that challenged or broke down your positive outlook. Try to identify the moments when you felt your attitude shifting and emotions like anger, self-pity, fear, or anxiety taking hold. What parts of the situation were outside your control? What things could you have changed?

....

....

....

....

....

....

....

....

....

....

"Any concern too small to be turned into a prayer
is too small to be made into a burden."
—Corrie ten Boom

Prepare for Recovery Barriers

Whether internal or external, there are barriers to recovery that can trigger relapse. Over time, character defects such as rationalization, denial, minimization, and the need for instant gratification can lessen your resolve to abstain and weaken your spirituality. External factors such as high-risk situations or events also build barriers to recovery.

To keep your recovery intact and diffuse potential triggers, keep turning your character defects over to your Higher Power. Continue to embrace the powerlessness you acknowledged in Step One.

Identifying barriers is the first step in overcoming them. Write down all the internal and external barriers to your recovery that you are currently experiencing.

"Sobriety is my Higher Power's gift to me. What I do with my sobriety is my gift to my Higher Power and others."

Try a Walking Meditation

Meditation doesn't have to be stationary. Find a quiet, calming place where you can walk, such as a park. Some places even have a labyrinth—a large circle composed of concentric paths—designed for walking meditation. The goal is to walk deliberately, slowly, and mindfully.

Try this, and pay deep attention to how your feet feel as they touch the ground, heel first. Notice sounds when you walk meditatively. If you see a beautiful object, stop and study it. Take a moment to marvel at how wonderfully things are made in nature. Be aware of your breathing. If intrusive thoughts come, let them pass like clouds passing through the sky.

Try a walking meditation today and describe the experience below.

....

....

....

....

....

....

....

....

....

....

"Meditation is knowing without thinking."
—Adapted from Voltaire

Understand How Anger Affects Addiction

Unresolved anger or resentment can leave you spiritually void and threaten your recovery. Looking outward, you think other people, places, and things make you angry, which allows you to hold on to resentment and avoid making changes. You might have anger issues if you

- are often impatient
- think others always do things wrong
- feel that to get something done right, you have to do it yourself
- feel the need to prove yourself
- complain a lot
- are often frustrated
- cannot "go with the flow"
- are often disrespectful of those with less power
- have frequent outbursts of temper
- feel your needs are minimized or ignored

Review this list and identify what pertains to you. Write positive affirmations for each feeling or action as a way to begin acting "as if," such as "I am a patient, loving person."

....

....

....

....

....

*"The alcoholic is only human. Alcoholics are . . . often faced with conditions
that arouse anger, but we need not be ignorant of the potential destructiveness
of unexamined anger or the inroads its impulses can make upon recovery."*
—*The Little Red Book*

Make a Miracle

What does it take to make a miracle? Faith and willingness. You can experience a miracle every time you give up your ego's perspective about something that is bothering you. It's very hard to do at first. It's human nature to want to control what your boss, spouse, or children think of you on any given day. It's normal to want every other driver on the road to drive as you do. Being right has been important to you. After all, doesn't it define how worthy you are?

When you let go of your ego and give control to your Higher Power, amazing things can happen. All it takes is the willingness you learned about in Step Six. It's hard to "let go and let God" at first, but with practice, you will discover how freeing it is to trust your Higher Power as the expert.

What miracles—coincidences, transformations, moments of grace, or answered prayers—have you experienced since you entered recovery? List them, and then thank your Higher Power for guiding you. Take a moment to give yourself some credit for working hard to let go of control.

....

....

....

....

....

....

....

"It is the function of our A.A. program to produce modern miracles."
—*Twenty-Four Hours a Day,* August 7

Stay Aware of Denial

What are your patterns for denial? Do you minimize the impact of your behavior on others? Are there amends you should make but keep putting off? Each of the Steps offers an opportunity to deal with denial, as you truthfully admit the toll your addiction has taken and work diligently to take responsibility for your actions.

Strict honesty is the best antidote for denial. Read what pages 328–337 in *Alcoholics Anonymous* say about denial. Repeat Steps Four and Five as often as needed to be honest in all areas of your life. Write down some things you can do to combat denial and be more honest.

....

....

....

....

....

....

....

....

....

....

....

"A half truth is a whole lie."
—Yiddish Proverb

Evaluate Your Recovery

How well are you working the Steps and connecting with others? Which of the following strategies are helping you work your recovery program?

- attending Twelve Step meetings regularly
- arriving early at meetings and welcoming newcomers
- reading Twelve Step literature
- talking to your sponsor at least once a week
- applying the Twelve Steps to your life daily
- spending time in prayer or meditation
- practicing honesty
- being willing to learn and grow in recovery

Identifying the ideas and activities that keep you grounded in recovery can help you maintain sobriety. Take some time to list the ideas, activities, and situations that keep you connected to recovery.

....

....

....

....

....

....

....

"Keep coming back. It works if you work it."

Celebrate Yourself

You build self-esteem when you practice self-acceptance and acknowledge your abilities and accomplishments. Reflecting on your positive traits is not about resting on your laurels; it is about understanding and utilizing your self-worth.

To strengthen your self-esteem, describe a few things you are really good at or that you like about yourself. Then write down some challenges you have taken on in recovery and how you felt after you accomplished these things.

Finally, make a list of the things about yourself you struggle to accept. In spite of these things, celebrate the amazing work in progress that you are today.

"I am a good person, and I am becoming better every day.
I will not define myself by my flaws."

Forgive Yourself

Consider this story from a thirty-four-year-old recovering heroin addict: "When I started working the Steps, I realized that guilt and shame had been dragging me down for years. I've finally learned the difference between guilt and shame. Guilt is feeling bad about something you've done, but shame is feeling bad about who you are. You can do something about guilt: admit the wrongs, apologize for them, and take corrective action. Shame is harder to fix. It goes hand in hand with being secretive and defensive. You have to learn to accept yourself and love yourself just as you are. You are doing your best right now, and you'll continue to do your best in the future."

Is there any shame that you are holding on to? Do you continue to blame yourself for things that happened in the past? Describe the one thing that shames you the most. It might be the one thing in your life that you would change, if you could. Write it down. Forgive yourself. It helps if you realize that you were doing the best you could do at the time. You are doing your best—even when you fail.

"*Most folks are about as happy as they make up their minds to be.*"
—Abraham Lincoln

Take Responsibility

Consider what one recovering person had to say about blame: "The guilt trips I laid on my spouse, parents, children, friends, and co-workers did nothing to change my sadness, anger, or frustration. I turned my fear outward in rage and blame because I couldn't take responsibility for my part in the situation. I felt like a failure already, and I just couldn't take one more ounce of defeat. Blaming others became my daily reaction to painful feelings. My sponsor challenged me to admit that I'm human, cut myself a little slack, and start taking responsibility for my own life. My sponsor accepted me and didn't think I was a bad person, even though I had my doubts about my own character. It took awhile, but when I started to accept myself and my faults, real growth began to happen."

Describe times when you've blamed others because you were afraid to face your own fears or accept responsibility for your own actions. What might you have done differently?

....

....

....

....

....

....

....

....

....

....

"It's sometimes easier to believe that other people, places, and things make us angry than to take responsibility for our own part in the situation."

Keep Focusing on Acceptance

When you clean up "your side of the street," your relationships benefit. Prayer and meditation can help improve your view of yourself and your relationship with others. These spiritual practices are powerful tools to help you accept others and understand how your Higher Power sees them. Acceptance begins as you start trusting others, acknowledge your role in a situation, and let go of resentments.

Center yourself and write down names of the people who are important to you. Meditate on this list to gain greater acceptance of these individuals. For example, you might think, "I will allow my daughter to be who she is. I will see the good in her every day." Now write your own name on the list and meditate on greater acceptance of yourself. Envy no one for who he or she is, and don't compare yourself to others. Celebrate you!

....

....

....

....

....

....

....

....

"We do not try to impose our wills on those who differ from us . . .
We do not have all the answers. We are not better than other good people.
We live the best way we can and we allow others to do likewise.
Am I willing to live and let live?"
—*Twenty-Four Hours a Day,* September 6

Congratulations for working on Step Eleven! You are beginning to find peace in spirituality. If you notice your old ways and thoughts resurfacing, go back and review the lessons you learned in this Step.

Embrace the Journey

DAY 336 TO DAY 365

Carry the Message

Step Twelve: "Having had a spiritual awakening as the result of these steps, we tried to carry this message to alcoholics, and to practice these principles in all our affairs."

"Carrying the message" is one of the best ways to solidify your recovery, which is why Step Twelve is one of the most important of the Steps. Your "spiritual awakening" does not need to be sudden or mystical; it can happen gradually. It begins with your admissions in Step One and continues through the other Steps as you courageously look within yourself and begin to make amends.

Step Twelve asks you to share the gift of your recovery. This keeps you spiritually grounded as you live the Steps and become a good example for others who struggle to recover. Remember to carry the message by "attraction rather than promotion." You cannot force someone to heed what you are sharing; the choice to recover is theirs, just as it was yours.

Describe in your own words what Step Twelve means to you.

....

....

....

....

....

....

....

....

....

....

"You can't keep it without giving it away."

Identify Areas of Growth

Ongoing growth in recovery is a rewarding, but often challenging, experience. Along with positive change, you may also be realizing that recovery doesn't solve everything. You may still struggle in your relationships with family, friends, or co-workers, or you might still be experiencing financial troubles or work difficulties.

You have already made significant changes. Trust that other changes will occur as you grow stronger in your recovery. Celebrate the progress you have already made. Take a moment and describe what you feel is your biggest area of growth.

....

....

....

....

....

....

....

....

....

....

....

"We are in relationships with imperfect people, just as we are imperfect."

Practice Recovery Principles

To "practice these principles in all our affairs" means to be genuine—to be your recovering self at home, at work, at play, and when you are alone with your thoughts, hopes, and fears. Strive to be honest with yourself, your Higher Power, and others. Practice trusting yourself, your Higher Power, and others. Surrender your ego and let your Higher Power direct you. Finally, share the lessons you have learned with those who still struggle to gain sobriety and join you on the path to recovery.

Meditate quietly, and then describe in your own words what it means to you to "practice these principles" in all your affairs. Are you your best recovering self in all aspects of your life?

....

....

....

....

....

....

....

....

....

....

"In recovery, practice doesn't mean perfection, but it should mean progress."

Surrender Your Fears

It is normal to have fears, even after almost a year of recovery. It's important to realize that most of your fears never happen. Facing fear can be difficult, but you don't have to do this alone. Your Higher Power can help, as can others in recovery. Monitor your fears by answering the following questions:

- What am I so worried might happen?
- What am I telling myself that makes me even more upset?
- What is the worst thing that could happen if this fear came true?
- From zero to ten, how would I rank my anxiety?
- What is the evidence that this could happen?
- From zero to ten, how likely is it that this will happen?
- If the worst happens, could I learn to deal with it?
- How could I cope?
- What is a more likely outcome?
- From zero to ten, how would I rank my anxiety now?

....

....

....

....

....

....

....

"Our antidote for fear is faith . . . in God as we understand Him."
—*The Little Red Book*

Live with More Gratitude

Have you ever heard someone say, "I'm a grateful alcoholic"? It seems like a strange concept, but in spite of the challenges you face, good things are coming your way. Maybe you have a new closeness and trust with your children, spouse, or friends. Perhaps you notice that you're not as anxious. Your level of gratitude reflects your ability to recognize and appreciate the goodness and grace in your life. Beginning and ending your day by practicing gratitude will restore your vitality and allow you a deeper (or perhaps newfound) sense of spirituality.

Practice gratitude today by listing some things or people in your life that you are grateful for. Describe a few ways you can express your gratitude. Discuss them with your sponsor, or talk with others in recovery for more ideas.

....

....

....

....

....

....

....

....

....

*"In the final analysis, it is through the grace of God
that any real change in human personality takes place."*
—*Twenty-Four Hours a Day,* March 6

Rebuild Family Trust

It may take time for your parents, spouse or partner, and children to trust you again, but be patient and allow them to express whatever they feel. Rebuilding trust can be stressful, so make sure you get support from recovery group members. Keep your goals realistic and give things time. Remember that your most important goal is to stay clean and sober. Go to meetings and stay in contact with your sponsor. Get enough food, rest, and exercise. The best way to rebuild your kids' trust is to let them see you in healthy recovery.

Ask your spouse how he or she coped while you were using. Ask your children the ways in which they parented themselves. Do you feel guilt or shame? Can you forgive yourself so you can move forward?

....

....

....

....

....

....

....

....

*"[My children] have given me a chance for companionship
that I had completely missed. I am their father or their mother now . . .
I am part of my home now."*
—Twenty-Four Hours a Day, *October 29*

Prepare for Good Things

Life is a preparation for something better to come. Your Higher Power has a grand plan for your life, far beyond what you can imagine now. Prepare for good things by practicing the Twelve Steps in your daily life. Be patient, open, and willing. Do your part and leave the rest up to your Higher Power.

Are you ready to have your Higher Power remove your character defects so that you can make room for good things? You may want to heal a struggling relationship; be a better parent, employee, or student; or experience happiness in small daily acts of kindness. Describe some of the good things you would like to experience in your life.

....

....

....

....

....

....

....

....

....

....

"All I have seen teaches me to trust the Creator for all I have not seen."
—Ralph Waldo Emerson

Explore Your Emotions

At this point in your recovery, it's normal to face challenging emotions. As you continue in recovery, you will get better at seeing emotions for what they are: a temporary state of being. You will get better at accepting that you will sometimes feel angry, sometimes happy, sometimes fearful. You can't always control or change your emotions. What you can do is change how you react. Start trying to let life's emotions roll over you. Practice being peaceful in the midst of fear or anger. Let these emotions pass like an ocean wave—intense at first, but then gone quickly.

Use this journal to describe and track your emotional and spiritual progress. When you look back, you will be able to see patterns in the way you react to life's challenges.

Describe some challenging emotions you've encountered since you've been sober. What happened to trigger the feelings? How did you react? What does this tell you about yourself? Is your reaction in line with your values? Could you have reacted in a better way? How can you change for the better?

....

....

....

....

....

....

....

....

"Positive actions speak louder than hasty reactions."

Spread Laughter

Think back over the last couple of weeks. Did you laugh? Did you make others laugh? If not, how could you plan for activities that will let you lighten up and see the comedy in life?

Laughter is good for the soul, and you do deserve to be happy. It can be hard to laugh or even smile, especially if you're having a tough week. Ask your sponsor or other friends in recovery how they have fun and how they lighten up. Go to a meeting and strike up a conversation with someone who has a good sense of humor. Laughter is contagious, and you might find it easier to laugh with someone who does it a lot.

Remember a time you felt very light and happy. Write down a description of the circumstances and how you felt. Can you start to imagine being happier in recovery than with the false happiness of using?

"If it's sanity you are after, there is no recipe like laughter."
—Henry Elliot

Carry the Message to Friends

Part of Step Twelve is to carry the message of recovery to other addicts. Let your friends know you're getting sober, and be ready to tell them why you are in recovery. For example, explain that if you kept using, you risked losing your job or your spouse. Ask them whether they're willing to do things with you that don't involve alcohol or other drugs.

Carry the message as Step Twelve asks, but realize you don't need to save all of your friends who still use. They may not understand addiction, or they may pressure you to keep using. You are only responsible for carrying the message; you are not responsible for the results. Always remember that your own recovery comes first. If spending time with a certain friend might threaten your recovery, you may need to end that friendship.

If you have using friends who are open to the message of recovery, begin to think about ways you could tell them about your experience working the Twelve Steps. Do this carefully, with the help of a sponsor or friend in recovery.

"We cannot share AA with alcoholics who reject our help.
It is pointless to try. We drop them for a while but leave the AA door open,
so they may call later if they have a change of heart."
—The Little Red Book

Stay Aware of Character Defects

It's not easy to acknowledge and keep on top of your weaknesses, but recovery requires that you do just that. The founders of Alcoholics Anonymous knew from their own experience how, unguarded, new character defects can creep into an addict's life. They knew how old defects could reappear, disguised as other things. You might mask self-centeredness in boredom, or hide intolerance with a self-righteous attitude. You might unwittingly replace low self-esteem with a new haughtiness as you grow more comfortable in your recovery.

Take a moment and meditate on your recent actions and reactions. Describe any new personality flaws you notice, or old qualities that have appeared in new forms. Ask your Higher Power to remove these defects, and consider discussing them with your sponsor or a recovery friend.

....

....

....

....

....

....

....

....

....

"When one door of happiness closes, another opens; but often we look so long at the closed door that we do not see the one which has been opened for us."
—Helen Keller

Keep Working Step Twelve

Pages 89–103 in *Alcoholics Anonymous* say you can help someone who is struggling with addiction by

- teaming up with a fellow Twelve Step member to talk to the person in private
- sharing your own experiences
- speaking of addiction as a disease
- stressing the spiritual nature of recovery
- describing the Twelve Steps and their purposes

The most convincing way you can carry the message is by setting a good example of what it means to be a person in recovery. You can also be of service by

- visiting new sponsees
- regularly attending meetings and sharing
- calling on members who might be hospitalized for chemical dependency
- phoning new members
- staying after meetings to talk to new members
- encouraging others to read the Big Book
- lending recovery literature to interested people
- talking to others to explain addiction and recovery
- leading meetings

Don't feel you need to save everyone who uses, but list ways in which you can carry the message.

....

....

....

....

"It helps me to help others."

Watch Out for Complacency

The danger of achieving a comfortable level of sobriety is thinking that you have "arrived"—that you have overcome your addiction and you don't have to worry about it anymore. The truth is that you are only a drink or hit away from danger. The spiritual focus that has helped you achieve a reprieve from the disease of addiction is the same focus you need to maintain your sobriety. Your spirituality reminds you that you are powerless—that you are not God. Review Step Eleven and pages 85–88 in *Alcoholics Anonymous*, which describe how to maintain a spiritual focus throughout your day.

Describe some practical ways you can maintain your spiritual focus every day.

....

....

....

....

....

....

....

....

....

....

"No one knows what he can do till he tries."
—Publilius Syrus

Keep Taking a Personal Inventory

Addiction is a clever, powerful disease that can use your own complacency as a reason to relapse. You need to be as wary when you are doing well as when you are not doing well. Part of working Step Ten is about asking others how you are doing. This teaches you humility and helps you realize that you are not always the best person to be taking your own personal inventory. Even people with twenty years in recovery still need to perform a Step Ten daily inventory to keep on track.

Make a commitment to set up a regular time to do your daily personal inventory with a supportive person, such as your sponsor or a recovery friend. Record how it feels to ask another person for this type of honest feedback. How is this an exercise in humility for you?

....

....

....

....

....

....

....

....

....

"It is unwise to be too sure of one's own wisdom. It is healthy to be reminded that the strongest might weaken and the wisest might err."
—Mohandas Gandhi

Deal with Unresolved Anger

Feeling anger is not the problem; the real culprit is *unresolved* anger. To protect your recovery, keep reminding yourself that you alone are responsible for how you feel. Step Four requires you to take a hard look at yourself, with all your assets and liabilities. This personal inventory helps release you from the unresolved anger and resentment that blocks you from your Higher Power. When you practice true honesty and learn humility, you lessen the power the past has over your life, and you are better able to let go of unresolved anger.

Keep a journal for several days, and describe times when you got angry. Identify your anger triggers, and describe how you acted in response to the situation. (Did you exchange harsh words? Did you give a dirty look or make a sarcastic comment?) List three other ways you could have responded to the situation that would result in a more positive outcome.

"Holding on to anger is like grasping a hot coal with the intent of throwing it at someone else; you are the one who gets burned."
—Buddha

Pamper Yourself

It may seem like an indulgence, but treating your body right involves more than just eating well or exercising. You deserve a gift to yourself for the hard work you are doing in recovery, and it can be fun to treat yourself to something healthy that you wouldn't ordinarily do.

Go to a massage therapist and get your anxious kinks worked out. Go to a chiropractor and get your back straightened out. Find a spiritual healer. Doing healthy things for your body is a gift that keeps on giving.

Write down how you feel right now. Which healthy activities would make you feel better?

....

....

....

....

....

....

....

....

....

"I offer you peace. I offer you love. I offer you friendship. I see your beauty.
I hear your need. I feel your feelings. My wisdom flows from the
Highest Source. I salute that Source in you."
—Mohandas Gandhi

Give Thanks for Courage

Now that you are almost through your first year of recovery, you may have discovered that you approach fear differently. You have a better understanding about what causes certain fears and which parts of yourself are threatened when you are afraid. This understanding enables you to sort which fears you will meet head-on and which you can let go of completely. In the process, your courage keeps growing.

Review the fears inventory that you began early in your recovery. How have your fears changed or lessened? Is it becoming easier to access courage? Take a moment to thank your Higher Power for giving you courage to make it this far in your recovery journey.

"There are two ways to live your life. One is as though nothing is a miracle.
The other is as though everything is a miracle."
—Albert Einstein

Consider Becoming a Sponsor

Helping others with their addiction strengthens your recovery by moving you from complacency into action and service. Now that you are nearing one year in recovery, you can consider being a sponsor for someone. Before becoming a sponsor, you should have

- a solid foundation (at least one year) in your recovery program
- an excellent relationship with your own sponsor
- thoroughly worked Steps One through Five
- a thorough knowledge of the Big Book and the Twelve Steps and Twelve Traditions
- attended and continue to attend Twelve Step meetings regularly

As a sponsor, your knowledge and experience will help your sponsee stay sober and evolve in recovery. You aren't expected to have all the answers, and you aren't responsible for the choices your sponsee makes. If you run into challenges, you can turn to the Big Book, your own sponsor, your Higher Power, or other people in recovery.

Try to imagine yourself being a sponsor to someone else. Describe what the challenges and benefits would be. Discuss these with your sponsor.

....

....

....

....

....

....

....

"Give and you shall receive."

Connect with Your Higher Power in Nature

Sometimes the most sacred places can be found outdoors. If you're feeling low or having trouble connecting with your Higher Power, try going for a walk. Walk deliberately and meditate, paying attention to the wonder in nature that surrounds you. Pause by a lake or riverbank, or relax in a park. Even a cemetery offers an opportunity for quiet contemplation in a place of beauty. Breathe deeply and get in touch with your senses. Feel the breeze, the warmth of the sun, the texture of the grass.

Take your journal along and record your observations and feelings. If you want, write a letter of thanksgiving to your Higher Power. When you get back, describe your experience.

"I only went out for a walk and finally concluded to stay out till sundown,
for going out, I found, was really going in."
—John Muir

Prepare Your Heart for Today

As you prepare your heart and mind to have positive, healthy thoughts and emotions, give your day and its decisions to your Higher Power, relinquishing your will and your need to control all that goes on in your life. It's important that you set aside your own will, motives, and ambitions each day. To do this, try the following prayer: "Help me set aside what I think I know about _____, so I can be teachable today."

Describe how using this prayer may improve your day and the decisions you make.

....

....

....

....

....

....

....

....

....

....

....

"I don't have all the answers, but my Higher Power does."

Find a Spiritual Mentor

You discovered the hard way that drugs are not God and cannot give you the peace and serenity you long for. By letting go of your self-will and trusting in a power greater than yourself, you opened the door to true spirituality. It's thrilling to realize the tranquility you desire is a prayer away. Through an ongoing and daily relationship with your Higher Power, you gain abundance and joy.

But it may be hard to maintain constant contact with your Higher Power without a little outside help. A spiritual mentor who understands Twelve Step recovery can often help you improve your relationship with your Higher Power. A spiritual mentor listens, offers guidance, and may ask you to read materials or complete exercises. He or she could come from any sort of spiritual background, such as someone from your church, a Native American holy person, or a Buddhist monk.

Who do you think would make a good spiritual mentor? How can you go about contacting that person?

....

....

....

....

....

....

....

....

"Pray and let God worry."
—Martin Luther

Learn More about Sponsorship

Sponsorship should not be entered into or ended without a lot of thought, prayer, and guidance from your own sponsor and your Higher Power. Sponsoring others should never put your own recovery in jeopardy or lessen its priority in your life. Both you and your sponsee should continue to grow in recovery, and if your sponsee refuses to work the Steps or commit to recovery, you can reconsider sponsorship.

All sponsors make occasional mistakes because they are human. The important thing is how you handle a mistake. Be sure to promptly admit it, and then make amends and talk to your sponsor about how to avoid similar mistakes in the future. Although you can discuss this with your sponsor, respect confidentiality and ask your sponsee's permission before sharing personal information.

Interview your own sponsor and ask for candid comments about the challenges and rewards of sponsorship. How could sponsorship strengthen your recovery? Write down the name of one person of your same gender that you would consider sponsoring in the next year.

....

....

....

....

....

....

....

....

"SPONSOR = Sober Person Offering Newcomers Suggestions On Recovery"

Stay Diligent

At this point in your recovery, you may be feeling happy, joyous, and free. You deserve it; you are finally learning to live in a way that works!

On the other hand, it's also common to struggle with complacency at this point. Maybe you're becoming bored with meetings. Maybe you think you've got everything under control because things in your life are going reasonably well. Maybe you think you don't need to work your program anymore.

In order to avoid a relapse, continue to work your recovery program and the Twelve Steps. Recovery is a lot like walking up and down on an escalator. There is no such thing as standing still.

Describe any ways you have felt complacent about recovery this week.

....

....

....

....

....

....

....

....

....

....

"We are not so interested in what we are as in what we are becoming."
—*Twenty-Four Hours a Day,* November 24

Reflect on Life

Recovery is not something you finish, like a test or a race. But it's still important to evaluate your progress. Celebrate and take credit where you are succeeding. Be just as fearless in examining areas where you need more work. Don't look at these as failures; they are only opportunities for you to become more successful.

Take some time to reflect on all you've learned and done during the past few months. Recognize the things that are going well and take steps to them. Take a look at the list below. It represents the main areas of your life.

- family life
- spiritual self
- financial health
- the way you spend your free time
- physical health
- friendships
- sex life
- job

Describe how you feel about these areas of your life. Identify things that you can do daily to improve.

....

....

....

....

....

"Change and growth take place when a person has risked himself
and dares to become involved with experimenting with his own life."
—Herbert Otto

Set Life Goals

Recovering people are cautioned not to dwell on the past or obsess about the future, but an ongoing daily inventory helps you assess how you are doing at this point in your journey. Think about your goals and dreams for a moment. Write down what you would like to achieve in the upcoming months and years. Break down these goals into small, achievable tasks, and be open to the lessons you can learn as you set out to accomplish them. What can you do today to move forward? Share your goals and dreams with your sponsor or a supportive family member, and ask these people to check in with you to see how you are doing.

"When it is obvious that goals cannot be reached,
don't adjust the goals, adjust the action steps."
—Confucius

Continue to Live a Life of Recovery

If you make a genuine, honest, and sincere effort to follow the Twelve Step program to the best of your ability, you will have all the tools you need to continue your journey of recovery for a lifetime. But you have to keep those tools sharpened and in good repair in order to ensure their effectiveness. One way to do this is by regularly attending meetings—remembering that you go to meetings for others as well as for yourself.

After your next meeting, resolve to have a friendly talk with someone, especially with a newcomer or someone who appears to be having trouble living the program. Listen attentively to what they say, and encourage them to read the Big Book and call their sponsor for guidance. Carrying the message of recovery to others is a great way to practice living the program.

Describe how you feel when you encourage others in their recovery. How does it strengthen your own recovery?

....

....

....

....

....

....

....

....

"The benefits of Twelve Step living enlarge as we share them with others."
—*The Little Red Book*

Take a Look at the New You

By this time in recovery, you're probably noticing that you're becoming a different person than the one you described when you first told your story. You may have related some horrific, hysterical, embarrassing, or painful tales of your using days, but now these stories may bore you. Instead, you are creating new stories as you move forward in recovery and look at the world with clear eyes and an open heart.

Describe how your story has changed since you entered recovery. If you want, try using the phrase "I used to _____, but now I _____" and launch your writing from there.

....

....

....

....

....

....

....

....

....

....

....

"Happiness is looking into a mirror and liking what you see."

Strengthen Sober Connections

Now that you've spent many months in your recovery journey, reflect for a moment on what keeps you going. What ideas, activities, and situations best connect you to sobriety? Is there a special person you rely on when you feel particularly vulnerable? What strategies do you have in place during those times?

Review your relapse response plan to remind yourself of your high-risk situations and feelings. Are these still current for you? Take a moment to answer the questions posed above and write down the things or people that help keep you strong in sobriety. Has this list changed since you first entered recovery?

....

....

....

....

....

....

....

....

....

....

"Our Higher Power gave us a kit of spiritual tools;
it's up to us to use them to build a durable shelter."

Live with Awareness

Congratulations! You are about to complete your first year as a recovering person. You have learned an enormous amount about being a spiritual person who practices the lessons of the Twelve Steps each day. But, like a one-year-old who toddles into his or her second year, you still need to reach out for occasional help in order to keep your balance. You still need to take life one careful step at a time as you continue to develop and grow strong in recovery.

Keep writing in your journal. Keep in close contact with your sponsor. Don't forget to go to meetings. The things that have gotten you this far in recovery are the things that will help you stay in recovery—the armor that will protect you as you go forward from here.

List some of your most important recovery tools, and then write an affirmation about your intentions to use them as you continue your recovery journey.

....

....

....

....

....

....

....

....

....

"We must think sober to live sober."
—*The Little Red Book*

Continue the Recovery Journey

In the last few months, you have learned that recovery is not a "sobriety program." Instead, it's a program of spiritual growth that not only provides a reprieve from the disease of addiction but also enriches your life. In the last few months, it's likely that you have grown spiritually. You're not perfect—none of us are—but you are learning to recognize and let go of your character flaws and be honest and open with yourself and others. You have learned that you are not God, that you can't control everything in life. You may still struggle with letting go of control, but you are learning that your Higher Power really will guide you, if you allow it. All things in your life must flow out from this spiritual core.

Consider this story from an alcoholic with three years of sobriety: "During my first year of recovery, I thought it was all about staying sober, but I found out that it's really so much more than that. Sobriety is only the beginning of the journey. During year two, I realized that recovery was more about my spiritual transformation and becoming the person I was always meant to be."

Describe the person you are meant to be. In what ways are you being successful in recovery? In what ways are you still struggling? What could you do to overcome these struggles?

....

....

....

....

....

....

....

"Decide what you want, decide what you are willing to exchange for it.
Establish your priorities and go to work."
—H. L. Hunt

Congratulations for working on Step Twelve! You are beginning to embrace the journey. If you notice your old ways and thoughts resurfacing, go back and review the lessons you learned in this Step.

Conclusion

Congratulations! You've made it through a year of recovery. Plan to do something special to acknowledge all the hard work you've done and the goals you've reached.

Recovery is a lifelong process, so don't get complacent. Even with all the progress you have made, it is crucial that you continue to work your recovery program each and every day. Success in life can be just as dangerous to your recovery as failure. The biggest mistake recovering people make is believing they have overcome their addiction. If you find yourself thinking this way, talk to your sponsor or a supportive, sober friend. Revisit Step One by reminding yourself that you are still powerless over the disease of addiction. If you find old, negative thoughts and behaviors resurfacing, take immediate steps to remove them so you don't start using again. Protect your sobriety fiercely, stay away from "slippery" situations, and stay on top of stress.

Remember to take a daily inventory, go to meetings, and keep sharing your recovery with others. Avoid returning to habits that harm you and your relationships, such as lying, blaming, rationalizing, or carrying resentments. Stay connected with your sponsor and supportive friends and family. When the time is right, consider becoming a sponsor yourself. Take care of yourself by taking some time each day to pray, meditate, exercise, or just sit quietly.

Continue to chart your progress by revising this journal from time to time, and notice the thoughts and feelings you recorded during your first year of recovery. Celebrate your growth as you look back at where you were in those first days, weeks, and months of recovery. See how far you've come and how much you've learned. With your Higher Power, you will always be safe and protected. If you stumble from time to time, know that others in recovery who love and support you are there to help.

"Kites and airplanes rise against the wind. In climbing up a high mountain,
we need the stony crags and rough places to aid us in our climb.
So your weakness can become an asset if you will face it, examine it,
and trace it to its origin. Set it in the very center of your mind."
—*Twenty-Four Hours a Day*, June 25

A New Day, A New Life: The Basics of Recovery
Video Discussion Questions

If alcohol and other drugs are undermining your best efforts at creating a healthy, rewarding life, turn to the video for *A New Day, A New Life.* It offers straight talk from others in recovery. They share the principles that will help you transform your life and begin true recovery from the disease of addiction.

After viewing the video, use the following questions to prompt a discussion with your sponsor, recovery group, or supportive family and friends. Each question includes a reference to a day in the journal where you can find more information and answers to these questions.

1. Brain science tells us that addiction is not a matter of strength, moral character, willpower, or weakness. It has to do with brain chemistry and the way your brain is "wired." Describe the disease of addiction in you own words, using your own experiences. *(Day 4: Understand the Science of Addiction)*

2. Recovering people often say that their whole life depends on not taking that first drink or hit—that they have to stay sober one day at a time until it becomes a habit. What does this mean to you? *(Day 12: Stay Away from All Mood-Altering Substances)*

3. Recovery is a group activity. What does this saying mean to you? What does it mean to "find strength in numbers" when you attend Twelve Step meetings such as Alcoholics Anonymous (AA) or Narcotics Anonymous (NA)? *(Day 29: Keep Surrendering)*

4. How can teaming up with a supportive sponsor help you change, improve, and grow stronger than you've ever been? *(Day 3: Find a Sponsor)*

5. Describe your idea of a Higher Power. How can your Higher Power help you achieve sobriety? *(Day 14: Find a Higher Power)*

6. Why is it important to avoid all the people, places, and things that could trigger you to start using alcohol and other drugs? *(Day 5: Plan Your Day)*